MW01058613

# The Pocket Book of Bible Prayers

Introduced and Compiled by
**David E. Rosage**
with
**Sister Marietta Darby, H.P.B.**

**SERVANT BOOKS**
Ann Arbor, Michigan

Cover design by Michael Andaloro
Cover photograph by Y. Brown/FPG

Published by Servant Books
P.O. Box 8617
Ann Arbor, Michigan 48107

Printed in the United States of America
ISBN 0-89283-320-3

87 88 89 90  10 9 8 7 6 5 4 3 2 1

# Contents

# Introduction

FOR SOME YEARS NOW we have been reaping a rich harvest of fruits accruing from the Second Vatican Council. One of the precious blessings we are enjoying is the refocusing of our attention on the word of God as found in the Scriptures. We are gradually coming to appreciate the Bible not only as the source of revelation and as a history of God's dealing with his people, but now we are recognizing the Scriptures more and more as God's communicating with each one of us personally and individually.

Our approach to the Bible is rapidly changing from a regard of it as only a compendium of doctrines, truths, and rules of conduct to an attitude of devotional listening to what the Lord is saying to us. With the psalmist we can say, "I will hear what God proclaims" (Ps 85:9).

In brief, the Scriptures are now recognized as an inexhaustible fountain of inspiration and motivation leading us into prayer. The words of Scripture form a pathway to a deeper awareness and a richer appreciation of God as our provident Father, of Jesus as our Savior and Redeemer, and of the Holy Spirit as our Divine Sanctifier.

Using the words of Scripture to energize our prayer, our vision becomes more cosmic, reaching far above our ordinary limitations. Praying with Scripture is like a window through which we get a little glimpse of the divine. It is the doorway through which we enter into union with the Triune God.

## Why This Anthology

This anthology is a collection of many of the powerful prayers found in various books of the Bible. These prayers have been assembled into a handbook of scriptural prayers readily available to those who are inundated with the duties of every day. The preoccupations of modern living afford little time to explore the sacred text in order to compile one's own selections.

We have tried to categorize these prayers to respond to the mood in which the reader may be at a given moment or to meet particular needs that one may have at a certain time—be it a plea in distress, an expression of thanksgiving, or perhaps a petition seeking mercy, enlightenment, reassurance, or direction.

Under each of the thirty-eight headings in Part II are listed some scriptural prayers that will hopefully meet the needs and desires of the reader in prayer. Such divisions are almost arbitrary since many of these prayers, especially the psalms, have several different themes. Some prayers begin with a lengthy prayer of praise and thanksgiving to God and suddenly switch into a desperate plea for help. Some of the psalms even give the impression that they are two or more separate prayers welded into one. For example, Psalm 19 consists of two parts: in the first part we hear the sun singing the glories of the Creator, while in the second section the psalmist praises God's moral code and prays for the grace to keep it. We find similar examples in Psalms 31, 68, and 102.

The same is true of the varying prayer moods and themes in some of the other prayers found in the Bible. However, under each heading you will find a great deal of similarity in the themes.

## *How to Use This Book*

The reader can find inspiration by simply reading this handbook from cover to cover. Or, more to our purpose, the table of contents can be used to help one find prayers for a given mood or need. Or again, the index at the back of the book will enable the reader to find particular passages or psalms. Perhaps one would want to read all the prayers from the Old Testament, from the New Testament, or from the Psalms.

It would be profitable from time to time to pray with pen or pencil in hand in order to underline a verse, a phrase, or a key word that attracts our attention. This procedure will not only help our concentration, but it will also enable us to return to the same passage in the future. Repetition helps us form habits of prayer.

Another beneficial technique is to keep a journal of the words, phrases, expressions, or verses that appeal to us. Writing them in a notebook will deepen their meaning for us and impress them more securely on our memory.

God himself tells us of the transforming power of his word: "So shall my word be / that goes forth from my mouth: / It shall not return to me void, / but shall do my will, / achieving the end for which I sent it" (Is 55:11).

In the same chapter, the Lord also admonishes us: "Come to me heedfully, / listen, that you may have life" (Is 55:3).

As we strive to come to him heedfully and listen, his word will achieve the end for which he sent it. This is our purpose and prayer in compiling this handbook. May our efforts lead all of us closer to the Lord who loves us so dearly.

# Part I

# Praying with God's Word

ONE

# Prayers in the Bible

THE APOSTLES WERE CLOSELY ASSOCIATED with Jesus, yet they had to admit that they did not know how to pray. One day after Jesus had finished praying, they asked him, "Lord, teach us to pray" (Lk 11:1).

St. Paul reminds us rather emphatically that we too do not know how to pray, but the Holy Spirit will teach us: "The Spirit too helps us in our weakness, for we do not know how to pray as we ought" (Rom 8:26). One of the ways in which the Spirit teaches us to pray is by leading us through the pages of Scripture and pointing out various prayers formulated by the inspired writers.

Even though we may be separated by centuries from the devout, prayerful heroes of the Bible, their prayers are still appropriate and adaptable to our own times. Basically we have the same reasons to raise our voices in praise and thanksgiving to our all-good God. Likewise, our needs are quite similar to the needs of those men and women of long ago.

Since God is not hemmed in by time and space, our relationship with him is cast in the eternal now. He is

3

immutable, always aware and alert to our needs. Our relationship of Creator to creature is unchangeable.

Let us examine just a few of the prayers that are so adaptable to our own circumstances. We will find many more of these prayers under the various headings in Part II.

At times we may be faced with a difficult task. We may feel totally inadequate to cope with a certain situation, to assume a responsibility, or to make an important decision. Solomon found himself in a similar situation when he became king. His prayer can readily become our own. We too need an understanding heart. Listen and pray with Solomon as he implores God's help:

"O Lord, my God, you have made me, your servant, king to succeed my father David; but I am a mere youth, not knowing at all how to act. I serve you in the midst of the people whom you have chosen, a people so vast that it cannot be numbered or counted. Give your servant, therefore, an understanding heart to judge your people and to distinguish right from wrong. For who is able to govern this vast people of yours?" (1 Kgs 3:7-9)

We can make the prayer of the prophet Habakkuk our own when we want God to manifest his loving concern in our lives and to renew his wondrous deeds in a given situation. Such a prayer will renew our own confidence and trust: "O Lord, I have heard your renown, / and feared, O Lord, your work. / In the course of the years revive it, / in the course of the years make it known; / in your wrath remember compassion!" (Hb 3:2).

The prayers of the New Testament seem even more appropriate for our daily needs. Listen to Jesus pray: "Father, Lord of heaven and earth, to you I offer praise; for what you have hidden from the learned and the clever you have revealed to the merest children" (Mt 11:25).

Such a prayer will transform our hearts to listen to the Lord with humility and a simple faith.

As we hear the distraught father pray, "I do believe! Help my lack of trust!" (Mk 9:24), our own confidence and trust in God will be greatly increased. And who of us cannot identify with the tax collector in the temple as he pleads, "O God, be merciful to me, a sinner" (Lk 18:13)?

We may find it difficult to forgive and forget at times. If we listen and pray with Jesus, realizing that he was praying for us also, we will be better able to forgive those who might have injured or scoffed at us: "Father, forgive them; they do not know what they are doing" (Lk 23:34).

These are but a few examples of the prayers from the Scriptures that will be found throughout this volume. They will not only lead us into prayer but will have a powerful transforming effect on us.

The prayers in the Bible are not only profound prayers in themselves, but they also serve as avenues leading us into other forms of prayer, especially vocal, meditative, and contemplative prayer.

## Vocal Prayer

One of the great fruits of vocal prayer is the support, encouragement, and reassurance it gives us throughout our work-a-day world. Such prayers help us in raising our minds and hearts above the mundane and aiding us to "be intent on things above rather than on things of earth" (Col 3:2). Scriptural prayers guide us in expressing to God our thoughts and feelings of awe and reverence, of adoration and worship, of praise and thanksgiving. How eloquently they express our desires for mercy and compassion, for forgiveness and healing! We can also find our own needs spoken powerfully in these scriptural prayers as we present our petitions before our caring and concerned God.

## Meditation

Meditation is also an excellent form of prayer. It is a rational process in which we consider some of the revealed truths about God or his divine attributes, such as his infinite goodness and his enduring love. The psalms and other scriptural prayers are an inexhaustible fountain of inspiration for meditative prayer.

## Prayer of the Heart

Even more enriching is the prayer of the heart which emanates from these inspired prayers. Biblical prayers enable us to enter into a listening posture conducive to contemplative prayer. As we read the words of these prayers, we should be on the alert to find a resting place on a word or phrase that brings us into an awareness of the presence and love of God. We will want to linger there to bask in the sunshine of his presence. When that happens, we need not read the remaining portion of the prayer but may rest, simply content to be with the Lord. Jesus must have included this method of prayer when he urged us, "Live on in my love" (Jn 15:9).

## *Gold Mine of Prayer*

This anthology is a compilation of only a few of the prayers verbalized and recorded by some of the great people who were called to a special role in God's plan of salvation and are recorded in the pages of Scripture. In addition to these prayers, there are countless passages in the Bible that are rich sources for our personal prayer; these words and expressions may inspire us to respond to the Lord with our own vocal prayer. Many times they will lead us into meditation and contemplation.

When we hear the Lord saying to us, "You are precious in my eyes and glorious, and I love you" (Is 43:4), we will naturally be drawn to whisper in our heart something like, "Thank you for loving me," or, "I love you too."

The words of Scripture also help us to form proper attitudes. By way of an example, when we hear our loving Father say, "I know well the plans I have in mind for you, plans for your welfare, not for woe! plans to give you a future full of hope" (Jer 29:11), we will find it much easier to trust him and to accept whatever comes our way.

In the New Testament there is an abundance of texts that will transform our minds and hearts. What reassurance St. John gives us when he writes, "Yes, God so loved the world / that he gave his only Son, / that whoever believes in him may not die / but may have eternal life" (Jn 3:16).

What love flows from the heart of Jesus when he assures us, "As the Father has loved me, / so I have loved you. / Live on in my love" (Jn 15:9).

Or again, "There is no greater love than this: / to lay down one's life for one's friends" (Jn 15:13).

A lifetime is too short for us to begin to comprehend

our loving, gracious, compassionate, benevolent Father together with the redeeming, healing, forgiving love of Jesus and the dynamic, sanctifying love of the Holy Spirit.

# TWO

# Prayers in the Psalms

WHEN CONSIDERING THE PRAYERS OF SCRIPTURE, one cannot leave out the Psalter. This collection of 150 psalms, inspired by the Holy Spirit, can guide us into a richer, more personal relationship with the Lord. The characteristic piety of the psalms is God-centered. It is often expressed in dialogue form.

The devotion expressed in the psalms is of a rather simple character. The Hebrews loved concrete expressions. They had little talent for abstractions, but they knew how to express eternity in terms of time, and transcendence in terms of distance.

Like all prayer, the psalms arise out of life and are intimately bound up with life. They portray concrete situations. A great variety of prayers are therefore expressed in the psalms—praise, petition, adoration, and so on.

Many of the psalms are spontaneous prayers crying out in every kind of distress: illness, false accusation, imprisonment, exile, danger, mental anguish, temptation.

The seven Penitential Psalms (Ps 6, 32, 38, 51, 102, 130, 143) deal with the essential evil—sinfulness. In them the sinner acknowledges his guilt and begs for forgiveness and mercy. Usually he is confident that a compassionate God will grant his requests. Psalm 51 is a typical example: "I acknowledge my offense, / and my sin is before me always. . . . / a heart contrite and humbled, O God, you will not spurn" (Ps 51:5, 19).

Fifteen songs of praise were chanted by the happy pilgrims on their way to the temple. They are called the Psalms of Ascent (Ps 120-134). Some thirty-five psalms are prayers of adoration, worship, and reverence. These psalms occur frequently in the liturgy.

## On Our Journey

The psalms keep us focused on God, and they lead us on our journey to him. God spoke to the psalmist through many signs; he does the same for us:

**1. Creation manifests the might and power of God.** He is present in creation. For the Hebrew, God was present in the thunder, lightning, clouds, and roaring of the sea. The happenings of nature were often personified: "Let the rivers clap their hands, / the mountains shout with them for joy" (Ps 98:8).

**2. The psalmist recognizes the presence of God in the history of his people.** History carries out God's designs and plans. God speaks through the events of history.

There is a truism that we cannot have a celebration without some kind of memorial. The psalms recall the events that call for celebration, such as the deliverance from the slavery of Egypt, which is celebrated each year in the Passover.

**3. In the psalms the temple is a sign of God's presence among his people.** For the Hebrews it was always a great joy to go to the temple. The temple was also the conservatory where many of the psalms were kept. A pilgrim could use these texts for his own prayer. Thus the psalms became a quasi-universal prayer formula.

**4. The Chosen People were themselves a sign of God's presence.** Repeatedly throughout the Old Testament we hear the Lord reminding the Israelites, "You shall be my people, and I will be your God" (Jer 11:4).

The Second Vatican Council also reminds us of the divine dwelling among us and in us: "Christ is always present in his Church... especially under the eucharistic species. By his power he is present in the sacraments. He is present in his word. He is present lastly when the Church prays and sings, for he promised: 'Where two or three are gathered together in my name, there am I in the midst of them' (Mt 18:20)" (*Constitution on the Liturgy*, Section #7).

Just as God's presence was evident among the Chosen People, so the Lord's presence is manifested in the Christian community. The psalmist begins the process of making us aware of God's presence. Jesus continues to bring us into this realization of his abiding presence. We are the new Israel.

**5. God's word was a sign of God's presence.** God made many extravagant promises to his people in his word. The psalmist on many occasions recalls the fidelity of God to every one of those promises. His word, then, is proof of his presence.

## Beyond Signs

The psalmist and all who prayed the psalms looked far beyond the external signs. They internalized the message the signs conveyed to them. The external signs stimulated faith in God's goodness, his kindness, his providential care.

These signs also generated a great hope in the hearts of the Israelites. The Jews prayed for salvation, peace, and blessings of every sort. As we pray the psalms, we can easily add a deeper spiritual dimension to these requests.

Today we find ourselves at home with the psalms as they lead us into a deeper reflection on our own interior life. The kingdom psalms are messianic and christocentric. The earthly king of the psalms is the symbol and foreshadowing of the kingship of the Messiah.

The church reverences and prays the psalms so extensively because of their christological character. Dom Athanasius Miller says, "All the human figures speaking in the Psalms somehow converge in Christ" (*The Songs of the Psalter*).

Jesus not only prayed the psalms but he also Christianized them, since he is the central prophetic figure in the psalms.

## Attitudinal Adjustments

Some persons may find it difficult to pray with the psalms for various reasons. Here are some of the most common obstacles to overcome.

**1. We may feel that we have attained a level of moral conduct and attitude far above that of the psalmists.** Some psalms may shock us by their unkindness, their vengefulness, and their imprecations. We must remember that these are expressions of deeply troubled souls whose horizons are still earthly. We, who have received Jesus' teaching on the love of God and love of neighbor, can appreciate all the more the life-style to which we have been called.

**2. We may feel that we have reached a theological level far above that which we find in the psalms.** It is true that when the psalmist prays for peace, blessing, life, and salvation, he is asking for a better life in this world. This should not create any problem for us, since we can easily transpose these ideals to the level of the spiritual gifts. This process was already begun in the Old Testament.

**3. Finally, we may wonder if the history of the psalmist's time is not past and gone, and therefore has little to offer us.** We can resolve that problem by remembering that the Bible is an account of the ups and downs of salvation history, which is often repeated in our own times. In the New Testament we discover that more than one-third of the quotations taken from the Old Testament are taken from the psalms. Surely they were integrated into our Christian way of life. Charles Pierre Peguy puts it very well: "Christ came to inherit a world already made, and yet he came to remake it totally."

The Psalter has contributed greatly to the history of salvation. If all the books of the Old Testament were lost and the only remaining book was the Psalter, we would still have a rather complete history of salvation.

Throughout the centuries the church has always prayed the psalms. They form the very heart of the Liturgy of the Hours and are used extensively in the eucharistic liturgy. Today the psalms are becoming more and more a part of the private prayer of many people.

## *Jesus Prayed the Psalms*

Jesus prayed the psalms with fervor and devotion; they are woven throughout his prayer. He came not to abolish ancient forms of prayer but to encourage and fulfill them. St. Augustine calls Jesus "the marvelous Singer of the Psalms."

When Jesus went up to the temple, he sang the Psalms of Ascent with the other pilgrims. His heart must have rejoiced with the people as they approached Mount Zion: "How lovely is your dwelling place, / O Lord of hosts! / My soul yearns and pines / for the courts of the Lord" (Ps 84:2-3).

At the Passover Jesus prayed the great Hallel Psalms with his people (Ps 113-118, 136, and 146-150): "Give thanks to the Lord, for he is good, / for his mercy endures forever" (Ps 136:1).

Jesus also prayed the psalms of the *anawim,* the simple, humble, lowly people. He was one of them. Did he not say, "I am gentle and humble of heart" (Mt 11:29)?

In his teaching Jesus often used the terminology of the psalms. He made his own the words of the just man who was persecuted: "Even my friend who had my trust / and partook of my bread, has raised his heel against me" (Ps 41:10).

On his deathbed on the cross Jesus prayed Psalm 22. It was a custom for a Jew to quote only the beginning of a prayer, indicating that he was making the whole prayer his own. When Jesus cried out, "My God, my God, why have you forsaken me?" it was not a cry of revolt, nor was it a cry of a person in despair. It was the Messiah declaring his trust in God. For Psalm 22 continues with praise of the Lord, who is always faithful to his people: "He has not hid his face from [the afflicted], but has heard, when he cried to him."

Jesus completed his final oblation in the words of the psalmist, "Into your hands I commend my spirit" (Ps 31:6).

In his first sermon after Pentecost St. Peter quoted the prophecy in Psalm 16:10 as proof of the resurrection: "Nor will you suffer your faithful one to undergo corruption."

## *The Psalms Speak of Jesus*

In the psalms we find a whole host of prophecies concerning the coming of the kingdom. The messianic and kingdom psalms are especially prophetic. These point to Jesus as the king, Lord, and Messiah to come. When Jesus was contending with his enemies who were contesting his authority, he pointed to the Scriptures for testimony to his mission: "Search the Scriptures in which you think you have eternal life—they also testify on my behalf" (Jn 5:39).

Jesus also singled out the psalms as giving testimony to him as redeemer: "'Recall those words I spoke to you when I was still with you: everything written about me in the law of Moses and the prophets and the psalms had to be fulfilled.' Then he opened their minds to the understanding of the Scriptures" (Lk 24:44-45).

In his discussion with the Pharisees Jesus asked a question that they could not answer: "What is your opinion about the Messiah? Whose son is he?" Then, quoting Psalm 110, Jesus said: "The Lord said to my Lord: 'Sit at my right hand till I make your enemies your footstool'" (see Mt 22:41-46).

We find the psalms quoted in Jesus' triumphal entry into Jerusalem on Palm Sunday: "Hosanna to the Son of David! / Blessed is he who comes in the name of the Lord! / Hosanna in the highest!" (Mt 21:9 quoting Ps 118:26).

Again, the evangelist quotes Psalm 8, which says, "Out of the mouths of babes and sucklings / you have fashioned praise because of your foes, / to silence the hostile and the vengeful" (Ps 8:3; see Mt 21:16).

We meet Jesus in the psalms that are used in the liturgy of the great feasts of the Lord: the Epiphany, the Ascension, the Transfiguration, Corpus Christi (Body and Blood of Christ), and the feast of Christ the King.

With Jesus let us become a "singer of the psalms."

# THREE

# Jesus Leads the Way

J ESUS WAS A MAN OF PRAYER. No one ever prayed as he did. His prayer always focused on the Father. He prayed with trust and confidence. He had very little time to teach his way of life and to establish his kingdom on earth; nevertheless, he spent much time in prayer. He often retired to a mountaintop, or to a desert place, or an olive grove to be alone with the Father. Jesus' life-style is a challenging model for us.

## *The Lord's Prayer*

At the time when Jesus walked the face of the earth, the rabbis were accustomed to summarizing their teaching in a prayer form, which their disciples learned and prayed from memory. Jesus did the same. He epitomized his teachings in a prayer form that we call the Lord's Prayer or the Our Father. This brief prayer sets forth a whole way of life for us.

When we pray, "Our Father in heaven," we acknowledge God as our heavenly Father. This recognition establishes an all-embracing relationship for our Christian living. If we relate to God as our Father, then we can accept our own dignity as his adopted children. Likewise, we can relate to others as truly our brothers and sisters, since we have a common Father. Furthermore, we can appreciate all creation as the handiwork of our Father.

Our petitions "your kingdom come" and "your will be done" simply strengthen and mature this relationship with him.

In the second portion of the Lord's Prayer we acknowledge the work of the whole Trinity. When we pray, "Give us today our daily bread," we are manifesting our dependence on our providing Father. "Forgive us the wrong we have done" is a recognition of Jesus as our Redeemer. When we plead, "Subject us not to the trial, but deliver us from the evil one," we are begging the Holy Spirit, the sanctifier, to help us ward off anything that would endanger our spiritual welfare, especially the enticements of the evil one.

With reflections such as these, it will require considerable time for us to pray the Our Father meditatively and contemplatively. Jesus says, "This is how you are to pray: 'Our Father in heaven, / hallowed be your name, / your kingdom come, / your will be done / on earth as it is in heaven. / Give us today our daily bread, / and forgive us the wrong we have done / as we forgive those who wrong us. / Subject us not to the trial / but deliver us from the evil one'" (Mt 6:9-13).

## How Did Jesus Pray?

*"In the days when he was in the flesh, he offered prayers and supplications with loud cries and tears to God, who was able to*

*save him from death, and he was heard because of his reverence"* (Heb 5:7).

## Jesus Prayed Liturgically

*In the temple:*
"His parents used to go every year to Jerusalem for the feast of the Passover, and when he was twelve they went up for the celebration as was their custom" (Lk 2:41-42).

*In the synagogue:*
"He came to Nazareth where he had been reared, and entering the synagogue on the sabbath as he was in the habit of doing, he stood up to do the reading" (Lk 4:16).

## Jesus Prayed in Solitude

"Rising early the next morning, he went off to a lonely place in the desert; there he was absorbed in prayer" (Mk 1:35).

"When he had sent them away, he went up on the mountain by himself to pray, remaining there alone as evening drew on" (Mt 14:23-24a; see Mk 6:46).

"He often retired to deserted places and prayed" (Lk 5:16).

"Then he went out to the mountain to pray, spending the night in communion with God" (Lk 6:12).

"One day when Jesus was praying in seclusion and the disciples were with him, he put the question to them, 'Who do the crowds say that I am?'" (Lk 9:18).

## Jesus Prayed on Location

*At his baptism:*

"When all the people were baptized, and Jesus was at prayer after likewise being baptized, the skies opened and the Holy Spirit descended on him in visible form like a dove. A voice from heaven was heard to say: 'You are my beloved Son. On you my favor rests'" (Lk 3:21-22).

*Blessing the loaves:*

"Jesus then took the loaves of bread, gave thanks, and passed them around to those reclining there; he did the same with the dried fish, as much as they wanted" (Jn 6:11).

"He took the seven loaves and the fish, and after giving thanks he broke them and gave them to the disciples, who in turn gave them to the crowds" (Mt 15:36).

"Then, taking the five loaves and the two fish, Jesus raised his eyes to heaven, pronounced a blessing, broke the loaves, and gave them to the disciples to distribute. He divided the two fish among all of them and they ate until they had their fill" (Mk 6:41-42).

*Before raising Lazarus:*

"They then took away the stone and Jesus looked upward and said: 'Father, I thank you for having heard me. / I know that you always hear me / but I have said this for the sake of the crowd, / that they may believe that you sent me'" (Jn 11:41-42).

*At the Transfiguration*
"About eight days after saying this he took Peter, John and James, and went up onto a mountain to pray. While he was praying, his face changed in appearance and his clothes became dazzlingly white" (Lk 9:28-29).

*With his disciples:*
"One day he was praying in a certain place. When he had finished, one of his disciples asked him, 'Lord, teach us to pray, as John taught his disciples'" (Lk 11:1).

*To praise his Father:*
"On one occasion Jesus spoke thus: 'Father, Lord of heaven and earth, to you I offer praise; for what you have hidden from the learned and the clever you have revealed to the merest children. Father, it is true. You have graciously willed it so'" (Mt 11:25-26).

## Jesus Prayed for Others

*For the children:*
"At one point, children were brought to him so that he could place his hands on them in prayer. The disciples began to scold them, but Jesus said, 'Let the children come to me. Do not hinder them. The kingdom of God belongs to such as these.' And he laid his hands on their heads before he left that place" (Mt 19:13-15).

*For Peter:*
"Simon, Simon! Remember that Satan has asked for you, to sift you all like wheat. But I have prayed for you that

your faith may never fail. You in turn must strengthen your brothers" (Lk 22:31-32).

*For the disciples:*
"For these I pray— / not for the world / but for these you have given me, / for they are really yours. / (Just as all that belongs to me is yours, / so all that belongs to you is mine.) / It is in them that I have been glorified. / I am in the world no more, / but these are in the world / as I come to you. / O Father most holy, / protect them with your name which you have given me / [that they may be one, even as we are one]. / As long as I was with them, / I guarded them with your name which you gave me. / I kept careful watch, / and not one of them was lost, / none but him who was destined to be lost— / in fulfillment of Scripture. / Now, however, I come to you; / I say all this while I am still in the world / that they may share my joy completely. / I gave them your word, / and the world has hated them for it; / they do not belong to the world / [any more than I belong to the world]. / I do not ask you to take them out of the world, / but to guard them from the evil one. / They are not of the world, / any more than I belong to the world. / Consecrate them by means of truth— / 'Your word is truth.' / As you have sent me into the world, / so I have sent them into the world; / I consecrate myself for their sakes now, / that they may be consecrated in truth" (Jn 17:9-19).

*For all believers:*
"I do not pray for them alone. / I pray also for those who will believe in me through their word, / that all may be one / as you, Father, are in me, and I in you; / I pray that they may be [one] in us, / that the world may believe that

you sent me. / I have given them the glory you gave me / that they may be one, as we are one— / I living in them, you living in me— / that their unity may be complete. / So shall the world know that you sent me, / and that you loved them as you loved me" (Jn 17:20-23).

*For our union with him:*
"Father, / all those you gave me / I would have in my company / where I am, / to see this glory of mine / which is your gift to me, / because of the love you bore me before the world began. / Just Father, / the world has not known you, / but I have known you; / and these men have known that you sent me. / To them I have revealed your name, / and I will continue to reveal it / so that your love for me may live in them, / and I may live in them" (Jn 17:24-26).

## Jesus Prayed

*For eternal life:*
"Father, the hour has come! / Give glory to your Son / that your Son may give glory to you, / inasmuch as you have given him authority over all mankind, / that he may bestow eternal life on those you gave him. / (Eternal life is this: / to know you, the only true God, / and him whom you have sent, Jesus Christ.) / I have given you glory on earth / by finishing the work you gave me to do. / Do you now, Father, give me glory at your side, / a glory I had with you before the world began" (Jn 17:1-5).

*At the Last Supper:*
"During the meal Jesus took bread, blessed it, broke it, and gave it to his disciples. 'Take this and eat it,' he said,

'this is my body.' Then he took a cup, gave thanks, and gave it to them. 'All of you must drink from it,' he said, 'for this is my blood, the blood of the covenant, to be poured out in behalf of many for the forgiveness of sins'" (Mt 26:26-28).

*In the garden:*
"He kept saying, *'Abba* (O Father), you have the power to do all things. Take this cup away from me. But let it be as you would have it, not as I'" (Mk 14:36).

"He advanced a little and fell prostrate in prayer. 'My Father, if it is possible, let this cup pass me by. Still, let it be as you would have it, not as I.' . . . Withdrawing a second time, he began to pray: 'My Father, if this cannot pass me by without my drinking it, your will be done!' . . . He left them again, withdrew somewhat, and began to pray a third time, saying the same words as before" (Mt 26:39, 42, 44).

"He withdrew from them about a stone's throw, then went down on his knees and prayed in these words: 'Father, if it is your will, take this cup from me; yet not my will but yours be done.' An angel then appeared to him from heaven to strengthen him. In his anguish he prayed with all the greater intensity, and his sweat became like drops of blood falling to the ground" (Lk 22:41-44).

*On his deathbed on the cross*
"Jesus said, 'Father, forgive them; they do not know what they are doing'" (Lk 23:34).

"Then toward midafternoon Jesus cried out in a loud tone, *'Eli, Eli, lema sabachthani?'* that is, 'My God, my God, why have you forsaken me?'" (Mt 27:46).

"Jesus uttered a loud cry and said, 'Father, into your hands I commend my spirit'" (Lk 23:46).

*After the Resurrection:*
"On the evening of that first day of the week, even though the disciples had locked the doors of the place where they were for fear of the Jews, Jesus came and stood before them. 'Peace be with you,' he said" (Jn 20:19).

## Jesus Prays Today

"Again I tell you, if two of you join your voices on earth to pray for anything whatever, it shall be granted you by my Father in heaven. Where two or three are gathered in my name, there am I in their midst" (Mt 18:19-20).

# Part II

# The Prayers

# The Prayers

## 1. To Begin Each Day with the Lord

Every morning sunrise offers us a new beginning. Everything awakens with a renewed freshness. Beginning the day with the Lord adds a luster and a lilt to our whole day. Jesus showed us the way: "Rising early the next morning, he went off to a lonely place in the desert; there he was absorbed in prayer" (Mk 1:35). Ask him to help you begin the day joyfully and spend it in loving service for others.

**For Guidance.** Now with you is Wisdom, who knows your works / and was present when you made the world; / Who understands what is pleasing in your eyes / and what is conformable with your commands. / Send her forth from your holy heavens / and from your glorious throne dispatch her / That she may be with me and work with me, / that I may know what is your pleasure. (Wis 9:9-10)

**For Strength.** O Lord, have pity on us, for you we wait. / Be our strength every morning, / our salvation in time of trouble! (Is 33:2)

**In His Presence.** "Master, how good it is for us to be here." (Lk 9:33)

**Invitation.** Come, Lord Jesus! (Rev 22:20)

**Hear My Voice.** *Hearken to my words, O Lord, / attend to my sighing. / Heed my call for help, / my king and my God! / To you I pray, O Lord; / at dawn you hear my voice; / at dawn I bring my plea expectantly before you.*

For you, O God, delight not in wickedness; / no evil man remains with you; / the arrogant may not stand in your sight. / You hate all evildoers; / you destroy all who speak falsehood; / The bloodthirsty and the deceitful / the Lord abhors.

But I, because of your abundant kindness, / will enter your house; / I will worship at your holy temple / in fear of you, O Lord; / Because of my enemies, guide me in your justice; / make straight your way before me.

For in their mouth there is no sincerity; / their heart teems with treacheries. / Their throat is an open grave; / they flatter with their tongue. / Punish them, O God; / let them fall by their own devices; / For their many sins, cast them out / because they have rebelled against you.

But let all who take refuge in you / be glad and exult forever. / Protect them, that you may be the joy / of those who love your name. / For you, O Lord, bless the just man; / you surround him with the shield of your good will. (Ps 5)

**Ever Present.** God is our refuge and our strength, / an ever-present help in distress. / Therefore we fear not, though the earth be shaken / and mountains plunge into the depths of the sea; / Though its waters rage and foam / and the mountains quake at its surging. / The Lord of hosts is with us; / our stronghold is the God of Jacob.

There is a stream whose runlets gladden the city of God, / the holy dwelling of the Most High. / God is in its midst; it shall not be disturbed. / God will help it at the break of dawn. / Though nations are in turmoil, kingdoms totter, / his voice resounds, the earth melts away, / The Lord of hosts is with us; / our stronghold is the God of Jacob.

Come! behold the deeds of the Lord, / the astounding things he has wrought on earth: / He has stopped wars to the end of the earth: / the bow he breaks; he splinters the spears; / he burns the shields with fire. / *Desist! and confess that I am God, / exalted among the nations, exalted upon the earth. / The Lord of hosts is with us; / our stronghold is the God of Jacob.* (Ps 46)

**Steadfast Heart.** *Have pity on me, O God; have pity on me, / for in you I take refuge. / In the shadow of your wings I take refuge, / till harm pass by. /* I call to God the Most High, / to God, my benefactor. / May he send from heaven and save me; / may he make those a reproach who trample upon me; / may God send his kindness and his faithfulness. / I lie prostrate in the midst of lions / which devour men; / Their teeth are spears and arrows, / their tongue is a sharp sword. / Be exalted above the heavens, O God; / above all the earth be your glory!

They have prepared a net for my feet; / they have bowed me down; / They have dug a pit before me, / but they fall into it. / My heart is steadfast, O God; my heart is steadfast; / I will sing and chant praise. / Awake, O my soul; awake, lyre and harp! / I will wake the dawn. / I will give thanks to you among the peoples, O Lord. / I will chant your praise among the nations, / For your kindness towers to the heavens, / and your faithfulness to the skies. / Be exalted above the heavens, O God; / above all the earth be your glory! (Ps 57)

**Give Thanks.** *It is good to give thanks to the Lord, / to sing praise to your name, Most High, / To proclaim your kindness at dawn / and your faithfulness throughout the night, /* With ten-stringed instrument and lyre, / with melody upon the harp. / For you make me glad, O Lord, by your deeds; / at the works of your hands I rejoice.

How great are your works, O Lord! / How very deep are your thoughts! / A senseless man knows not, / nor does a fool understand this. / Though the wicked flourish like grass / and all evildoers thrive, / They are destined for eternal destruction; / while you, O Lord, are the Most High forever.

For behold, your enemies, O Lord, / for behold, your enemies shall perish; / all evildoers shall be scattered. / You have exalted my horn like the wild bull's; / you have anointed me with rich oil. / And my eye has looked down upon my foes, / and my ears have heard of the fall of my wicked adversaries.

The just man shall flourish like the palm tree, / like a cedar of Lebanon shall he grow. / They that are planted in the house of the Lord / shall flourish in the courts of our God. / They shall bear fruit even in old age; /

vigorous and sturdy shall they be, / Declaring how just is the Lord, / my Rock, in whom there is no wrong. (Ps 92)

**Ready Heart.** *My heart is steadfast, O God; my heart is steadfast; / I will sing and chant praise. / Awake, O my soul; awake, lyre and harp; / I will wake the dawn. / I will give thanks to you among the peoples, O Lord; / I will chant your praise among the nations, / For your kindness towers to the heavens, / and your faithfulness to the skies. /* Be exulted above the heavens, O God; / over all the earth be your glory! / That your loved ones may escape, / help us by your right hand, and answer us.

God promised in his sanctuary: / "Exultantly I will apportion Shechem, / and measure off the valley of Succoth; / Mine is Gilead, and mine Manasseh, / Ephraim is the helmet for my head; Judah, my scepter; / Moab shall serve as my washbowl; / upon Edom I will set my shoe; / I will triumph over Philistia."

Who will bring me into the fortified city? / Who will lead me into Edom? / Have not you, O God, rejected us, / So that you go not forth, O God, with our armies? / Give us aid against the foe, / for worthless is the help of men. / Under God we shall do valiantly; / it is he who will tread down our foes. (Ps 108)

## 2. At Eventide

As the evening shadows lengthen, our mood becomes more relaxed and pensive. This is an ideal time to say thank you for the blessings of the day and to ask forgiveness for any faults and failures. Even as we "fall peacefully asleep" our prayer continues, for "I was sleeping, but my heart kept vigil" (Song 5:2a).

**Song of Thanksgiving.** "O Lord, my rock, my fortress, my deliverer, / my God, my rock of refuge! / My shield, the horn of my salvation, / my stronghold, my refuge, / my savior, from violence you keep me safe. / 'Praised be the Lord,' I exclaim, / and I am safe from my enemies...."

"The Lord rewarded me according to my justice; / according to the cleanness of my hands he requited me. / For I kept the ways of the Lord / and was not disloyal to my God. / For his ordinances were all present to me, / and his statutes I put not from me; / But I was wholehearted toward him, / and I was on my guard against guilt. / And the Lord requited me according to my justice, / according to my innocence in his sight.

"Toward the faithful you are faithful; / toward the wholehearted you are wholehearted; / Toward the sincere you are sincere; / but toward the crooked you are astute. / You save lowly people, / though on the lofty your eyes look down. / You are my lamp, O Lord! / O my God, you brighten the darkness about me." (2 Sm 22:2-4, 21-29)

**Dream Fulfilled.** "Now, Master, you can dismiss your servant in peace; / you have fulfilled your word. / For my eyes have witnessed your saving deed / displayed for all the peoples to see: / A revealing light to the Gentiles, / the glory of your people Israel." (Lk 2:29-32)

**Do Stay.** "Stay with us. It is nearly evening—the day is practically over." (Lk 24:29)

**Evening Examen.** *Hear, O Lord, a just suit; / attend to my outcry; / hearken to my prayer from lips without deceit. / From you let my judgment come; / your eyes behold what is right. / Though you test my heart, searching it in the night, / though you try me with fire, you shall find no malice in me. / My mouth has not transgressed after the manner of man; / according to the words of your lips I have kept the ways of the law.* / My steps have been steadfast in your paths, / my feet have not faltered. / I call upon you, for you will answer me, O God; / incline your ear to me; hear my word. / Show your wondrous kindness, / O savior of those who flee / from their foes to refuge at your right hand. / Keep me as the apple of your eye; / hide me in the shadow of your wings / from the wicked who use violence against me. / My ravenous enemies beset me; / they shut up their cruel hearts, / their mouths speak proudly. / Their steps even now surround me; / crouching to the ground, they fix their gaze, / Like lions hungry for prey, / like young lions lurking in hiding. / Rise, O Lord, confront them and cast them down; / rescue me by your sword from the wicked, / by your hand, O Lord, from mortal men: / From mortal men whose portion in life is in this world, / where with your treasures you fill their bellies. / Their sons are enriched / and bequeath their abundance to their little ones. / But I in justice shall behold your face; / on waking, I shall be content in your presence. (Ps 17)

**Outstretched Hands.** *Aloud to God I cry; / aloud to God, to hear me; / on the day of my distress I seek the Lord. / By night my hands are stretched out without flagging; / my soul refuses comfort. / When I remember God, I moan; / when I ponder, my spirit grows faint. / You keep my eyes watchful; / I am troubled and cannot speak. / I consider* the days of old; / the years long past I remember. / *In the night I meditate in my heart; / I ponder, and my spirit broods: / "Will the Lord reject forever / and nevermore be favorable? /* Will his kindness utterly cease, / his promise fail for all generations? / Has God forgotten pity? / Does he in anger withhold his compassion?" / And I say, "This is my sorrow, / that the right hand of the Most High is changed." / I remember the deeds of the Lord; / yes, I remember your wonders of old. / And I meditate on your works; / your exploits I ponder. / O God, your way is holy; / what great god is there like our God? / You are the God who works wonders; / among the peoples you have made known your power. / With your strong arm you redeemed your people, / the sons of Jacob and Joseph. / The waters saw you, O God; / the waters saw you and shuddered; / the very depths were troubled. / The clouds poured down water; / the skies gave forth their voice; / your arrows also sped abroad. / Your thunder resounded in the whirlwind; / your lightning illumined the world; / the earth quivered and quaked. / Through the sea was your way, / and your path through the deep waters, / though your footsteps were not seen. / You led your people like a flock / under the care of Moses and Aaron. (Ps 77)

**Universal Praise.** *Praise the Lord, all you nations; / glorify him, all you peoples! / For steadfast is his kindness toward us, / and the fidelity of the Lord endures forever.* (Ps 117)

**Night Watch.** *Come, bless the Lord, / all you servants of the Lord / Who stand in the house of the Lord / during the hours* *of night.* / Lift up your hands toward the sanctuary, / and bless the Lord. / May the Lord bless you from Zion, / the maker of heaven and earth. (Ps 134)

**Eyes Godward.** *O Lord, to you I call; hasten to me; / hearken to my voice when I call upon you. / Let my prayer come like incense before you; / the lifting up of my hands, like the evening sacrifice.* / O Lord, set a watch before my mouth, / a guard at the door of my lips. / Let not my heart incline to the evil / of engaging in deeds of wickedness / With men who are evildoers; / and let me not partake of their dainties. / Let the just man strike me; that is kindness; / let him reprove me; it is oil for the head, / Which my head shall not refuse, / but I will still pray under these afflictions. / Their judges were cast down over the crag, / and they heard how pleasant were my words. / As when a plowman breaks furrows in the field, / so their bones are strewn by the edge of the nether world. / For toward you, O God, my Lord, my eyes are turned; / in you I take refuge; strip me not of life. / Keep me from the trap they have set for me, / and from the snares of evildoers. / Let all the wicked fall, each into his own net, / while I escape. (Ps 141)

## 3. To Enrich Our Prayerful Spirit

Listening to the sounds of silence is an essential posture for meeting the Lord at the core of our being in prayer. He himself bids us, "Come to me heedfully, / listen, that you may have life" (Is 55:3). When life seems

drab and prayer seems dry, we can come to the Lord with
confidence, for he will bring forth "streams in the desert"
of our thirsty souls.

**Speak, Lord.** "Speak, Lord, for your servant is listening."
(1 Sm 3:9)

**A Prayerful Heart.** May God bless you and remember
his covenant. . . . May he give to all of you a heart to
worship him and to do his will readily and generously.
May he open your heart to his law and his commandments and grant you peace. May he hear your prayers, and
be reconciled to you, and never forsake you in time of
adversity. Even now we are praying for you here. (2 Mc
1:2-6)

**Lover of Souls.** For with you great strength abides
always; / who can resist the might of your arm? / Indeed,
before you the whole universe is as a grain from a balance,
/ or a drop of morning dew come down upon the earth. /
But you have mercy on all, because you can do all things;
/ and you overlook the sins of men that they may repent.
/ For you love all things that are / and loathe nothing
that you have made; / for what you hated, you would not
have fashioned. / And how could a thing remain, unless
you willed it; / or be preserved, had it not been called
forth by you? / But you spare all things, because they are
yours, O Lord and lover of souls, / for your imperishable
spirit is in all things! (Wis 11:21-12:1)

**Teach Us.** "Lord, teach us to pray." (Lk 11:1)

**Lord God.** "Mighty and wonderful are your works, / Lord God Almighty! / Righteous and true are your ways, / O King of the nations! / Who would dare refuse you honor, / or the glory due your name, O Lord? / Since you alone are holy, / all nations shall come / and worship in your presence. / Your mighty deeds are clearly seen." (Rv 15:3b-4)

**Wait for the Lord.** Be not vexed over evildoers, / nor jealous of those who do wrong; / For like grass they quickly wither, / and like green herbs they wilt. / Trust in the Lord and do good, / that you may dwell in the land and enjoy security. / *Take delight in the Lord, / and he will grant you your heart's requests. / Commit to the Lord your way; / trust in him, and he will act.* / He will make justice dawn for you like the light; / bright as the noonday shall be your vindication. / Leave it to the Lord, / and wait for him; / Be not vexed at the successful path / of the man who does malicious deeds. / Give up your anger, and forsake wrath; / be not vexed, it will only harm you. / For evildoers shall be cut off, / but those who wait for the Lord shall possess the land. / Yet a little while, and the wicked man shall be no more; / though you mark his place he will not be there. / But the meek shall possess the land, / they shall delight in abounding peace. / The wicked man plots against the just / and gnashes his teeth at them; / But the Lord laughs at him, / for he sees that his day is coming. / A sword the wicked draw; they bend their bow / to bring down the afflicted and the poor, / to slaughter those whose path is right. / But their swords shall pierce their own hearts, / and their bows shall be broken. / Better is the scanty store of the just / than the great wealth of the wicked, / For the power of the wicked shall be broken, / but the Lord supports the just. / The Lord watches over the lives of the wholehearted; / their inheritance lasts forever. / They are not put to shame in an evil time, / in days of famine they have plenty. / But the wicked perish, / and the enemies of the Lord, like the beauty of the meadows, / vanish; like smoke they vanish. / The wicked man borrows and does not repay; / the just man is kindly and gives, / But those whom he blesses shall possess the land, / while those he curses shall be cut off. / *By the Lord are the steps of a man made firm, / and he approves his way. / Though he fall, he does not lie prostrate, / for the hand of the Lord sustains him.* / Neither in my youth, nor now that I am old, / have I seen a just man forsaken / nor his descendants begging bread. / All the day he is kindly and lends, / and his descendants shall be blessed. / Turn from evil and do good, / that you may abide forever; / For the Lord loves what is right, / and forsakes not his faithful ones. / Criminals are destroyed, / and the posterity of the wicked is cut off. / The just shall possess the land / and dwell in it forever. / The mouth of the just man tells of wisdom / and his tongue utters what is right. / The law of his God is in his heart, / and his steps do not falter. / The wicked man spies on the just, / and seeks to slay him. / The Lord will not leave him in his power / nor let him be condemned when he is on trial. / Wait for the Lord, / and keep his way; / He will promote you to ownership of the land; / when the wicked are destroyed, you shall look on. / I saw a wicked man, fierce, / and stalwart as a flourishing, age-old tree. / Yet as I passed by, lo! he was no more; / I sought him, but he could not be found. / Watch the wholehearted man, and mark the upright; / for there is a future for the man of peace. / Sinners shall all alike be destroyed; / the future of the wicked shall be cut off. / The salvation of the just is from the Lord; / he is their refuge in time of distress. / And the Lord helps them and delivers them; / he delivers them from the wicked and saves them, / because they take refuge in him. (Ps 37)

**Call to Listen.** *Come, let us sing joyfully to the Lord; / let us acclaim the Rock of our salvation. / Let us greet him with thanksgiving; / let us joyfully sing psalms to him.* / For the Lord is a great God, / and a great king above all gods; / In his hands are the depths of the earth, / and the tops of the mountains are his. / His is the sea, for he has made it, / and the dry land, which his hands have formed. / *Come, let us bow down in worship; / let us kneel before the Lord who made us. / For he is our God, / and we are the people he shepherds, the flock he guides.* / O, that today you would hear his voice: / "Harden not your hearts as at Meribah, / as in the day of Massah in the desert, / Where your fathers tempted me; / they tested me though they had seen my works. / Forty years I loathed that generation, / and I said: They are a people of erring heart, / and they know not my ways. / Therefore I swore in my anger: / They shall not enter into my rest." (Ps 95)

**God's Goodness.** *I will give thanks to the Lord with all my heart / in the company and assembly of the just. / Great are the works of the Lord, / exquisite in all their delights.* / Majesty and glory are his work, / and his justice endures forever. / He has won renown for his wondrous deeds; / gracious and merciful is the Lord. / He has given food to those who fear him; / he will forever be mindful of his covenant. / He has made known to his people the power of his works, / giving them the inheritance of the nations. / The works of his hands are faithful and just; / sure are all his precepts, / Reliable forever and ever, / wrought in truth and equity. / He has sent deliverance to his people; / he has ratified his covenant forever; / holy and awesome is his name. / The fear of the Lord is the beginning of wisdom; / prudent are all who live by it. / His praise endures forever. (Ps 111)

**Childlike Trust.** O Lord, my heart is not proud, / nor are my eyes haughty; / I busy not myself with great things, / nor with things too sublime for me. / *Nay rather, I have stilled and quieted / my soul like a weaned child. / Like a weaned child on its mother's lap, / [so is my soul within me].* / O Israel, hope in the Lord, / both now and forever. (Ps 131)

**All-Knowing, Ever-Present.** O Lord, you have probed me and you know me; / you know when I sit and when I stand; / you understand my thoughts from afar. / My journeys and my rest you scrutinize, / with all my ways you are familiar. / Even before a word is on my tongue, / behold, O Lord, you know the whole of it. / Behind me and before, you hem me in / and rest your hand upon me. / Such knowledge is too wonderful for me; / too lofty for me to attain. / Where can I go from your spirit? / from your presence where can I flee? / If I go up to the heavens, you are there; / if I sink to the nether world, you are present there. / If I take the wings of the dawn, / if I settle at the farthest limits of the sea, / Even there your hand shall guide me, / and your right hand hold me fast. / If I say, "Surely the darkness shall hide me, / and night shall be my light"— / For you darkness itself is not dark, / and night shines as the day. / [Darkness and light are the same.] / Truly you have formed my inmost being; / you knit me in my mother's womb. / I give you thanks that I am fearfully, wonderfully made; / wonderful are your works. / My soul also you knew full well; / nor was my frame unknown to you / When I was made in secret, / when I was fashioned in the depths of the earth. / Your eyes have seen my actions; / in your book they are all written; / my days were limited before one of them existed. / How weighty are your designs, O God; / how vast the sum of them! / Were I to recount them, they would outnumber the sands; / did I reach the end of them, I should still be with you. / If only you would destroy the wicked, O God, / and the men of blood were to depart from me! / Wickedly they invoke your name; / your foes swear faithless oaths. / Do I not hate, O Lord, those who hate you? / Those who rise up against you do I not loathe? / With a deadly hatred I hate them; / they are my enemies. / *Probe me, O God, and know my heart; / try me, and know my thoughts; / See if my way is crooked, / and lead me in the way of old.* (Ps 139)

## 4. To Praise Our Loving Creator

"Since the creation of the world, invisible realities, God's eternal power and divinity, have become visible, recognized through the things he has made" (Rom 1:20). For the fauna and flora, for the sunshine and the rain, for things great and small, we give glory and praise. Above all we give thanks for the gift of life, which is only a prelude to the life that has no end.

**Sole Creator.** "It is you, O Lord, you are the only one; you made the heavens, the highest heavens and all their host, the earth and all that is upon it, the seas and all that is in them. To all of them you give life, and the heavenly hosts bow down before you." (Neh 9:6)

**Lord of Creation.** "O Lord of hosts, God of Israel, enthroned upon the cherubim! You alone are God over all the kingdoms of the earth. You have made the heavens and the earth." (Is 37:16)

**Mighty in Deeds.** Lord God, you have made heaven and earth by your great might, with your outstretched arm; nothing is impossible to you. You continue your kindness through a thousand generations. . . . O God, great and mighty, whose name is Lord of hosts, great in counsel, mighty in deed, whose eyes are open to all the ways of men, giving to each according to his ways, according to the fruit of his deeds. (Jer 32:17-19)

**Glorifying God.** Bless the Lord, all you works of the Lord, / praise and exalt him above all forever. / Angels of the Lord, bless the Lord, / praise and exalt him above all forever. / You heavens, bless the Lord, / praise and exalt him above all forever. / All you waters above the heavens, bless the Lord, / praise and exalt him above all forever. / All you hosts of the Lord, bless the Lord; / praise and exalt him above all forever.

Sun and moon, bless the Lord; / praise and exalt him above all forever. / Stars of heaven, bless the Lord; / praise and exalt him above all forever. / Every shower and dew, bless the Lord; / praise and exalt him above all forever. / All you winds, bless the Lord; / praise and exalt him above all forever. / Fire and heat, bless the Lord; / praise and exalt him above all forever. / [Cold and chill, bless the Lord; / praise and exalt him above all forever. / Dew and rain, bless the Lord; / praise and exalt him above all forever.] / Frost and chill, bless the Lord; / praise and exalt him above all forever. / Ice and snow, bless the Lord; / praise and exalt him above all forever.

Nights and days, bless the Lord; / praise and exalt him above all forever. / Light and darkness, bless the Lord; / praise and exalt him above all forever. / Lightnings and clouds, bless the Lord; / praise and exalt him above all forever. / Let the earth bless the Lord, / praise and exalt him above all forever. / Mountains and hills, bless the Lord; / praise and exalt him above all forever. / Everything growing from the earth, bless the Lord; / praise and exalt him above all forever.

You springs, bless the Lord; / praise and exalt him above all forever. / Seas and rivers, bless the Lord; / praise and exalt him above all forever. / You dolphins and all water creatures, bless the Lord; / praise and exalt him above all forever. / All you birds of the air, bless the Lord; / praise and exalt him above all forever. / All you beasts, wild and tame, bless the Lord; / praise and exalt him above all forever.

You sons of men, bless the Lord; / praise and exalt him above all forever. / O Israel, bless the Lord; / praise and exalt him above all forever. / Priests of the Lord, bless the Lord; / praise and exalt him above all forever. / Servants of the Lord, bless the Lord; / praise and exalt him above all forever. / Spirits and souls of the just, bless the Lord;

/ praise and exalt him above all forever. / Holy men of humble heart, bless the Lord; / praise and exalt him above all forever. (Dn 3:57-87)

**Worthy of Praise.** "O Lord our God, you are worthy / to receive glory and honor and power! / For you have created all things; / by your will they came to be and were made!" (Rv 4:11)

**What Is Man?** O Lord, our Lord, / how glorious is your name over all the earth! / You have exalted your majesty above the heavens. / Out of the mouths of babes and sucklings / you have fashioned praise because of your foes, / to silence the hostile and the vengeful. / *When I behold your heavens, the work of your fingers, / the moon and the stars which you set in place— / What is man that you should be mindful of him, / or the son of man that you should care for him?* / You have made him little less than the angels, / and crowned him with glory and honor. / You have given him rule over the works of your hands, / putting all things under his feet: / All sheep and oxen, / yes, and the beasts of the field, / The birds of the air, the fishes of the sea, / and whatever swims the paths of the seas. / O Lord, our Lord, / how glorious is your name over all the earth! (Ps 8)

**Hymn to the Creator.** *Bless the Lord, O my soul! / O Lord, my God, you are great indeed! / You are clothed with majesty and glory, / robed in light as with a cloak.* / You have spread out the heavens like a tent-cloth; / you have constructed your palace upon the waters. / You make the clouds your chariot; / you travel on the wings of the wind. / You make the winds your messengers, / and flaming fire your ministers. / You fixed the earth upon its foundation, / not to be moved forever; / With the ocean, as with a garment, you covered it; / above the mountains the waters stood. / At your rebuke they fled, / at the sound of your thunder they took to flight; / As the mountains rose, they went down the valleys / to the place you had fixed for them. / You set a limit they may not pass, / nor shall they cover the earth again. / You send forth springs into the watercourses / that wind among the mountains, / And give drink to every beast of the field, / till the wild asses quench their thirst. / Beside them the birds of heaven dwell; / from among the branches they send forth their song. / You water the mountains from your palace; / the earth is replete with the fruit of your works. / You raise grass for the cattle, / and vegetation for men's use, / Producing bread from the earth, / and wine to gladden men's hearts, / So that their faces gleam with oil, / and bread fortifies the hearts of men. / Well watered are the trees of the Lord, / the cedars of Lebanon, which he planted; / In them the birds build their nests; / fir trees are the home of the stork. / The high mountains are for wild goats; / the cliffs are a refuge for rock-badgers. / You made the moon to mark the seasons; / the sun knows the hour of its setting. / You bring darkness, and it is night; / then all the beasts of the forest roam about; / Young lions roar for the prey / and seek their food from God. / When the sun rises, they withdraw / and couch in their dens. / Man goes forth to his work / and to his tillage till the evening. / *How manifold are your works, O Lord! / In wisdom you have wrought them all— / the earth is full of your creatures;* / The sea also, great and wide, / in which are schools without number / of living things both small and great, / And where ships move about / with

Leviathan, which you formed to make sport of it. / They all look to you / to give them food in due time. / When you give it to them, they gather it; / when you open your hand, they are filled with good things. / If you hide your face, they are dismayed; / if you take away their breath, they perish / and return to their dust. / When you send forth your spirit, they are created, / and you renew the face of the earth. / *May the glory of the Lord endure forever; / may the Lord be glad in his works!* / He who looks upon the earth, and it trembles; / who touches the mountains, and they smoke! / I will sing to the Lord all my life; / I will sing praise to my God while I live. / Pleasing to him be my theme; / I will be glad in the Lord. / May sinners cease from the earth, / and may the wicked be no more. / Bless the Lord, O my soul! Alleluia. (Ps 104)

**Praising Our Creator.** *Praise the Lord from the heavens, / praise him in the heights;* / Praise him, all you his angels, / praise him, all you his hosts. / Praise him, sun and moon; / praise him, all you shining stars. / Praise him you highest heavens, / and you waters above the heavens. / Let them praise the name of the Lord, / for he commanded and they were created; / He established them forever and ever, / he gave them a duty which shall not pass away. / Praise the Lord from the earth, / you sea monsters and all depths; / Fire and hail, snow and mist, / storm winds that fulfill his word; / You mountains and all you hills, / you fruit trees and all you cedars; / You wild beasts and all tame animals, / you creeping things and you winged fowl. / Let the kings of the earth and all peoples, / the princes and all the judges of the earth, / Young men too, and maidens, / old men and boys, /

*Praise the name of the Lord, / for his name alone is exalted; / His majesty is above the earth and heaven, /* and he has lifted up the horn of his people. / Be this his praise from all his faithful ones, / from the children of Israel, the people close to him. Alleluia. (Ps 148)

## 5. *To Thank Our Providing Father*

How exciting is Jesus' reassurance: "Your heavenly Father knows all that you need" (Mt 6:32). To make sure we caught the message he says again: "As for you, every hair of your head has been counted; so do not be afraid of anything" (Mt 10:30-31). Every bit of oxygen for our 25,000 respirations daily, every morsel of food, every drop of water, has been provided by our gracious Father. How much more joyful life becomes when we know that he cares for us today and every day!

**David's Blessing.** "Blessed may you be, O Lord, / God of Israel our father, / from eternity to eternity.

"Yours, O Lord, are grandeur and power, / majesty, splendor, and glory. / For all in heaven and on earth is yours; / yours, O Lord, is the sovereignty; / you are exalted as head over all." (1 Chr 29:10b-11)

**Powerful Yet Merciful.** "A new hymn I will sing to my God. / O Lord, great are you and glorious, / wonderful in power and unsurpassable. / Let your every creature serve you; / for you spoke, and they were made, / You sent forth your spirit, and they were created; / no one can resist your word. / The mountains to their bases, and the seas, are shaken; / the rocks, like wax, melt before your glance. / But to those who fear you, / you are very merciful." (Jdt 16:13-15)

**Prophetic Canticle.** "Blessed be the Lord the God of Israel / because he has visited and ransomed his people. / He has raised a horn of saving strength for us / in the house of David his servant, / As he promised through the mouths of his holy ones, / the prophets of ancient times: / Salvation from our enemies / and from the hands of all our foes. / He has dealt mercifully with our fathers / and remembered the holy covenant he made, / The oath he swore to Abraham our father he would grant us: / that, rid of fear and delivered from the enemy, / We should serve him devoutly and through all our days / be holy in his sight. / And you, O child, shall be called / prophet of the Most High; / For you shall go before the Lord / to prepare straight paths for him, / Giving his people a knowledge of salvation / in freedom from their sins. / All this is the work of the kindness of our God; / he, the Dayspring, shall visit us in his mercy / To shine on those who sit in darkness / and in the shadow of death, / to guide our feet into the way of peace." (Lk 1:68-79)

**My Shepherd.** *The Lord is my shepherd; I shall not want.* / In verdant pastures he gives me repose; / Beside restful waters he leads me; / he refreshes my soul. / He guides me in right paths / for his name's sake. / Even though I walk in the dark valley / I fear no evil; for you are at my side / With your rod and your staff / that give me courage. / You spread the table before me / in the sight of my foes; / You anoint my head with oil; / my cup overflows. / *Only goodness and kindness follow me / all the days of my life; / And I shall dwell in the house of the Lord / for years to come.* (Ps 23)

**Bountiful Harvest.** To you we owe our hymn of praise, / O God, in Zion; / To you must vows be fulfilled, / you who hear prayers. / To you all flesh must come / because of wicked deeds. / We are overcome by our sins; / it is you who pardon them. / Happy the man you choose, and bring / to dwell in your courts. / May we be filled with the good things of your house, / the holy things of your temple! / With awe-inspiring deeds of justice you answer us, / O God our savior, / The hope of all the ends of the earth / and of the distant seas. / You set the mountains in place by your power, / you who are girt with might; / You still the roaring of the seas, / the roaring of their waves and the tumult of the peoples. / And the dwellers at the earth's ends are in fear at your marvels; / the farthest east and west you make resound with joy. / *You have visited the land and watered it; / greatly have you enriched it. / God's watercourses are filled; / you have prepared the grain. / Thus have you prepared the land: drenching its furrows, / breaking up its clods, / Softening it with showers, / blessing its yield. / You have crowned the year with your bounty, / and your paths overflow with a rich harvest;* / The untilled meadows overflow with it, / and rejoicing clothes the hills. / The fields are garmented with flocks / and the valleys blanketed with grain. / They shout and sing for joy. (Ps 65)

**Harvest Prayer.** May God have pity on us and bless us; / may he let his face shine upon us. / So may your way be known upon earth; / among all nations, your salvation. /

May the peoples praise you, O God; / may all the peoples praise you! / May the nations be glad and exult / because you rule the people in equity; / the nations on the earth you guide. / May the peoples praise you, O God; / may all the peoples praise you! / *The earth has yielded its fruits; / God, our God, has blessed us. / May God bless us, / and may all the ends of the earth fear him!* (Ps 67)

**Beneficent Father.** "Give thanks to the Lord, for he is good, / for his kindness endures forever!" / Thus let the redeemed of the Lord say, / those whom he has redeemed from the hand of the foe / And gathered from the lands, / from the east and the west, from the north and the south. / They went astray in the desert wilderness; / the way to an inhabited city they did not find. / Hungry and thirsty, / their life was wasting away within them. / They cried to the Lord in their distress; / from their straits he rescued them. / And he led them by a direct way / to reach an inhabited city. / *Let them give thanks to the Lord for his kindness / and his wondrous deeds to the children of men, / Because he satisfied the longing soul / and filled the hungry soul with good things.* / They dwelt in darkness and gloom, / bondsmen in want and in chains, / Because they had rebelled against the words of God / and scorned the counsel of the Most High. / And he humbled their hearts with trouble; / when they stumbled, there was no one to help them. / They cried to the Lord in their distress; / from their straits he rescued them. / And he led them forth from darkness and gloom / and broke their bonds asunder. / Let them give thanks to the Lord for his kindness / and his wondrous deeds to the children of men, / Because he shattered the gates of

brass / and burst the bars of iron. / Stricken because of
their wicked ways / and afflicted because of their sins, /
They loathed all manner of food, / so that they were near
the gates of death. / They cried to the Lord in their
distress; / from their straits he rescued them. / He sent
forth his word to heal them / and to snatch them from
destruction. / Let them give thanks to the Lord for his
kindness / and his wondrous deeds to the children of
men. / Let them make thank offerings / and declare his
works with shouts of joy. / They who sailed the sea in
ships, / trading on the deep waters, / These saw the
works of the Lord / and his wonders in the abyss. / His
command raised up a storm wind / which tossed its
waves on high. / They mounted up to heaven; they sank
to the depths; / their hearts melted away in their plight. /
They reeled and staggered like drunken men, / and all
their skill was swallowed up. / They cried to the Lord in
their distress; / from their straits he rescued them. / He
hushed the storm to a gentle breeze, / and the billows of
the sea were stilled; / They rejoiced that they were
calmed, / and he brought them to their desired haven. /
Let them give thanks to the Lord for his kindness / and
his wondrous deeds to the children of men. / Let them
extol him in the assembly of the people / and praise him
in the council of the elders. / He changed rivers into
desert, / water springs into thirsty ground, / Fruitful
land into salt marsh, / because of the wickedness of its
inhabitants. / *He changed the desert into pools of water, /
waterless land into water springs. / And there he settled the
hungry, / and they built a city to dwell in.* / They sowed
fields and planted vineyards, / and they obtained a
fruitful yield. / He blessed them, and they became very

many; / nor did he suffer their cattle to decrease. / And they dwindled and were brought low / through oppression, affliction and sorrow. / But he who pours out contempt upon princes, / and sends them astray through a trackless waste, / Lifted up the needy out of misery / and made the families numerous like flocks. / The upright see this and rejoice, / and all wickedness closes its mouth. / Who is wise enough to observe these things / and to understand the favors of the Lord? (Ps 107)

**Loving Kindness.** Praise the Lord, for he is good; / sing praise to our God, for he is gracious; / it is fitting to praise him. / The Lord rebuilds Jerusalem; / the dispersed of Israel he gathers. / He heals the brokenhearted / and binds up their wounds. / He tells the number of the stars; / he calls each by name. / Great is our Lord and mighty in power: / to his wisdom there is no limit. / The Lord sustains the lowly; / the wicked he casts to the ground. / *Sing to the Lord with thanksgiving; / sing praise with the harp to our God, / Who covers the heavens with clouds, / who provides rain for the earth; / Who makes grass sprout on the mountains / and herbs for the service of men; / Who gives food to the cattle, / and to the young ravens when they cry to him.* / In the strength of the steed he delights not, / nor is he pleased with the fleetness of men. / The Lord is pleased with those who fear him, / with those who hope for his kindness. / Glorify the Lord, O Jerusalem; / praise your God, O Zion. / For he has strengthened the bars of your gates; / he has blessed your children within you. / He has granted peace in your borders; / with the best of wheat he fills you. / He sends forth his command to the earth; / swiftly runs his word!

/ He spreads snow like wool; / frost he strews like ashes. / He scatters his hail like crumbs; / before his cold the waters freeze. / He sends his word and melts them; / he lets his breeze blow and the waters run. / He has proclaimed his word to Jacob, / his statutes and his ordinances to Israel. / He has not done thus for any other nation; / his ordinances he has not made known to them. Alleluia. (Ps 147)

## 6. To Acknowledge Our Sinfulness

Biblical men and women were straightforward in acknowledging their sinfulness before God. Can we make a humble acknowledgment of our wrongdoing without rationalizing? St. John says, "If we say, 'We are free of the guilt of sin,' we deceive ourselves; the truth is not to be found in us. But if we acknowledge our sins, he who is just can be trusted to forgive our sins and cleanse us from every wrong" (1 Jn 1:8-9).

**Shame and Confusion.** "My God, I am too ashamed and confounded to raise my face to you, O my God, for our wicked deeds are heaped up above our heads and our guilt reaches up to heaven.... O Lord, ... you are just.... Here we are before you in our sins. Because of all this, we can no longer stand in your presence." (Ezr 9:6, 15)

**We Know Our Offenses.** For our offenses before you are many, / our sins bear witness against us. / Yes, our offenses are present to us / and our crimes we know: / Transgressing, and denying the Lord, / turning back from following our God, / Threatening outrage, and apostasy, / uttering words of falsehood the heart has conceived. (Is 59:12-13)

**Many Rebellions.** Even though our crimes bear witness against us, / take action, O Lord, for the honor of your name— / Even though our rebellions are many, / though we have sinned against you. / O Hope of Israel, O Lord, / our savior in time of need! (Jer 14:7-8a)

**We Have Rebelled.** "We have sinned, been wicked and done evil; we have rebelled and departed from your commandments and your laws. We have not obeyed your servants the prophets, who spoke in your name to our kings, our princes, our fathers, and all the people of the land. Justice, O Lord, is on your side; we are shamefaced even to this day." (Dn 9:5-7a)

**Sinful Son.** "Father, I have sinned against God and against you; I no longer deserve to be called your son." (Lk 15:18)

**I Confess My Fault.** Happy is he whose fault is taken away, / whose sin is covered. / Happy the man to whom the Lord imputes not guilt, / in whose spirit there is no guile. / As long as I would not speak, my bones wasted away / with my groaning all the day, / For day and night your hand was heavy upon me; / my strength was dried up as by the heat of summer. / *Then I acknowledged my sin to you, / my guilt I covered not. / I said, "I confess my faults to the Lord," / and you took away the guilt of my sin.* / For this shall every faithful man pray to you / in time of stress. / Though deep waters overflow, / they shall not reach him.

/ You are my shelter; from distress you will preserve me; / with glad cries of freedom you will ring me round. / I will instruct you and show you the way you should walk; / I will counsel you, keeping my eye on you. / Be not senseless like horses or mules: / with bit and bridle their temper must be curbed, / else they will not come near you. / Many are the sorrows of the wicked, / but kindness surrounds him who trusts in the Lord. / Be glad in the Lord and rejoice, you just; / exult, all you upright of heart. (Ps 32)

**I Acknowledge My Offense.** Have mercy on me, O God, in your goodness; / in the greatness of your compassion wipe out my offense. / Thoroughly wash me from my guilt / and of my sin cleanse me. / *For I acknowledge my offense, / and my sin is before me always: / "Against you only have I sinned, / and done what is evil in your sight"— / That you may be justified in your sentence, / vindicated when you condemn.* / Indeed, in guilt was I born, / and in sin my mother conceived me; / Behold, you are pleased with sincerity of heart / and in my inmost being you teach me wisdom. / Cleanse me of sin with hyssop, that I may be purified; / wash me, and I shall be whiter than snow. / Let me hear the sounds of joy and gladness; / the bones you have crushed shall rejoice. / Turn away your face from my sins, / and blot out all my guilt. / *A clean heart create for me, O God, / and a steadfast spirit renew within me. / Cast me not out from your presence, / and your holy spirit take not from me. / Give me back the joy of your salvation, / and a willing spirit sustain in me.* / I will teach transgressors your ways, / and sinners shall return to you. / Free me from blood guilt, O God, my saving God; / then my tongue shall revel in your justice. / O Lord, open my lips, / and my mouth shall proclaim your praise. / For you are not pleased with sacrifices; / should I offer a holocaust, you would not accept it. / My sacrifice, O God, is a contrite spirit; / a heart contrite and humbled, O God, you will not spurn. / Be bountiful, O Lord, to Zion in your kindness / by rebuilding the walls of Jerusalem; / Then shall you be pleased with due sacrifices, / burnt offerings and holocausts; / then shall they offer up bullocks on your altar. (Ps 51)

**We Have Sinned.** Give thanks to the Lord, for he is good, / for his kindness endures forever. / Who can tell the mighty deeds of the Lord, / or proclaim all his praises? / Happy are they who observe what is right, / who do always what is just. / Remember me, O Lord, as you favor your people; / visit me with your saving help, / That I may see the prosperity of your chosen ones, / rejoice in the joy of your people, / and glory with your inheritance. / *We have sinned, we and our fathers; / we have committed crimes; we have done wrong.* / Our fathers in Egypt / considered not your wonders; / They remembered not your abundant kindness, / but rebelled against the Most High at the Red Sea. / Yet he saved them for his name's sake, / to make known his power. / He rebuked the Red Sea, and it was dried up, / and he led them through the deep as through a desert. / He saved them from hostile hands / and freed them from the hands of the enemy. / The waters covered their foes; / not one of them was left. / Then they believed his words / and sang his praises. / But soon they forgot his works; / they waited not for his counsel. / They gave way to craving in the desert / and tempted God in the wilderness. / He gave them what they asked / but sent a wasting disease against them. / They envied Moses in the camp, / and Aaron, the holy one of the Lord. / The earth opened and swallowed up Dathan, / and covered the faction of Abiram. / Fire broke out against their faction; / a flame consumed the wicked. / They made a calf in Horeb / and adored a molten image; / They exchanged their glory / for the image of a grass-eating bullock. / They forgot the God who had saved them, / who had done great deeds in Egypt, / Wondrous deeds in the land of Ham, / terrible things at the Red Sea. / Then he spoke of exterminating them, / but Moses, his chosen one, / Withstood him in the breach / to turn back his destructive wrath. / Yet they despised the desirable land; / they believed not his word. / They murmured in their tents, / and obeyed not the voice of the Lord. / Then with raised hand he swore against them / to let them perish in the desert, / To scatter their descendants among the nations, / and to disperse them over the lands. / And they submitted to the rites of Baal of Peor / and ate the sacrifices of dead gods. / They provoked him by their deeds, / and a plague attacked them. / Then Phinehas stood forth in judgment / and the plague was checked; / And it was imputed to him for merit / through all generations forever. / They angered him at the waters of Meribah, / and Moses fared ill on their account, / For they embittered his spirit, / and the rash utterance passed his lips. / They did not exterminate the peoples, / as the Lord had commanded them, / But mingled with the nations / and learned their works. / They served their idols, / which became a snare for them. / They sacrificed their sons / and their daughters to demons, / And they shed innocent blood, / the blood of their sons and their daughters, / Whom they sacrificed to the idols of Canaan, / desecrating the land with bloodshed; / They became defiled by their works, / and wanton in their crimes. / And the Lord grew angry with his people, / and abhorred his inheritance; / He gave them over into the hands of the nations, / and their foes ruled over them. / Their enemies oppressed them, / and they were humbled under their power. / Many times did he rescue them, / but they embittered him with their counsels / and were brought low by their guilt. / Yet he had regard for their affliction / when he heard their cry; / And for their sake he was mindful of his covenant / and relented, in his abundant kindness, / And he won for them compassion / from all who held them captive. / *Save us, O Lord, our God, / and gather us from among the nations, / That we may give thanks to your holy name / and glory in praising you.* / Blessed be the Lord, the God of Israel, through all eternity! / Let all the people say, Amen! Alleluia. (Ps 106)

## 7. To Ask for Mercy

The Hebrew word for God's mercy is like a huge umbrella embracing so many of his divine attributes—his kindness, forgiveness, pity, mercy. This gives us a clue to the immensity of his love. "God is rich in mercy; because of his great love for us he brought us to life with Christ when we were dead in sin. By this favor you were saved" (Eph 2:4-5). "So let us confidently approach the throne of grace to receive mercy and favor and to find help in time of need" (Heb 4:16).

**Rich in Mercy.** "You are a God of pardons, gracious and compassionate, slow to anger and rich in mercy; you did not forsake them.... Therefore you delivered them into the power of their enemies, who oppressed them. But in the time of their oppression they would cry out to you, and you would hear them from heaven, and according to your great mercy give them saviors to deliver them from the power of their enemies.... for you are a kind and merciful God." (Neh 9:17, 27, 31b)

**Blessed Be God.** "Blessed be God, / and praised be his great name, / and blessed be all his holy angels. / May his holy name be praised / throughout all the ages, / Because it was he who scourged me, / and it is he who has had mercy on me." (Tb 11:14b-15a)

**God of Mercy.** "Lord Almighty, God of Israel, afflicted souls and dismayed spirits call to you. Hear, O Lord, for you are a God of mercy; and have mercy on us, who have sinned against you." (Bar 3:1-2)

**Spare Us, O Lord.** "Spare, O Lord, your people, / and make not your heritage a reproach, / with the nations ruling over them! / Why should they say among the peoples, / 'Where is their God?'" (Jl 2:17)

**Have Pity.** "Lord, Son of David, have pity on us!" (Mt 20:30)

**Be Merciful.** "O God, be merciful to me, a sinner." (Lk 18:13)

**Like a Green Olive Tree.** Why do you glory in evil, / you champion of infamy? / All the day you plot harm; / your tongue is like a sharpened razor, you practiced deceiver! / You love evil rather than good, / falsehood rather than honest speech. / You love all that means ruin, / you of the deceitful tongue! / God himself shall demolish you; / forever he shall break you; / He shall pluck you from your tent, / and uproot you from the land of the living. / The just shall look on with awe; / then they shall laugh at him: / "This is the man who made not / God the source of his strength, / But put his trust in his great wealth, / and his strength in harmful plots." / *But I, like a green olive tree / in the house of God, / Trust in the kindness of God / forever and ever. / I will thank you always for what you have done, / and proclaim the goodness of your name / before your faithful ones.* (Ps 52)

**Mercy Unlimited.** Why, O God, have you cast us off forever? / Why does your anger smolder against the sheep of your pasture? / Remember your flock which you built up of old, / the tribe you redeemed as your inheritance, / Mount Zion, where you took up your abode. / Turn your steps toward the utter ruins; / toward all the damage the enemy has done in the sanctuary. / Your foes roar triumphantly in your shrine; / they have set up their tokens of victory. / They are like men coming up with axes to a clump of trees; / and now with chisel and hammer they hack at all its paneling. / They set your sanctuary on fire; / the place where your name abides they have razed and profaned. / They said in their hearts,

/ "Let us destroy them; / burn all the shrines of God in the land." / Deeds on our behalf we do not see; there is no prophet now, / and no one of us knows how long. . . . / How long, O God, shall the foe blaspheme? / Shall the enemy revile your name forever? / Why draw back your hand / and keep your right hand idle beneath your cloak? / Yet, O God, my king from of old, / you doer of saving deeds on earth, / You stirred up the sea by your might; / you smashed the heads of the dragons in the waters. / You crushed the heads of Leviathan, / and made food of him for the dolphins. / You released the springs and torrents; / you brought dry land out of the primeval waters. / Yours is the day, and yours the night; / you fashioned the moon and the sun. / You fixed all the limits of the land; / summer and winter you made. / Remember how the enemy has blasphemed you, O Lord, / and how a stupid people has reviled your name. / Give not to the vulture the life of your dove; / be not forever unmindful of the lives of your afflicted ones. / Look to your covenant, / for the hiding places in the land and the plains are full of violence. / *May the humble not retire in confusion; / may the afflicted and the poor praise your name. / Arise, O God; defend your cause; / remember how the fool blasphemes you day after day.* / Be not unmindful of the voice of your foes; / the uproar of those who rebel against you is unceasing. (Ps 74)

**Trust in His Mercy.** *O Lord, hear my prayer; / hearken to my pleading in your faithfulness; / in your justice answer me. / And enter not into judgment with your servant, / for before you no living man is just.* / For the enemy pursues me; / he has crushed my life to the ground; / he has left me dwelling in the dark, like those long dead. / And my spirit is faint within me, / my heart within me is appalled. / I remember the days of old; / I meditate on all your doings, / the works of your hands I ponder. / I stretch out my hands to you; / my soul thirsts for you like parched land. / Hasten to answer me, O Lord, / for my spirit fails me. / Hide not your face from me / lest I become like those who go down into the pit. / *At dawn let me hear of your kindness, / for in you I trust. / Show me the way in which I should walk, / for to you I lift up my soul.* / Rescue me from my enemies, O Lord, / for in you I hope. / Teach me to do your will, / for you are my God. / May your good spirit guide me / on level ground. / For your name's sake, O Lord, preserve me; / in your justice free me from distress, / And in your kindness destroy my enemies; / bring to nought all my foes, / for I am your servant. (Ps 143)

## 8. To Plead for Compassion

The English word *pity* does not adequately describe the emotion of God's heart toward his weak and needy creatures. *Compassion,* on the other hand, denotes the ability to put oneself in another person's place, something Jesus did so remarkably in the Incarnation. "Moved with compassion, Jesus touched their eyes, and immediately they could see; and they became his followers." (Mt 20:34)

**A Redeemed People.** In your mercy you led the people you redeemed; / in your strength you guided them to your holy dwelling. (Ex 15:13)

**Pardon Your People.** "Now then, let the power of my Lord be displayed in its greatness, even as you have said, 'The Lord is slow to anger and rich in kindness, forgiving wickedness and crime; yet not declaring the guilty guiltless, but punishing children to the third and fourth generation for their fathers' wickedness.' Pardon, then, the wickedness of this people in keeping with your great kindness." (Nm 14:17-19)

**Look Upon Us.** O Lord, you are our father; / we are the clay and you the potter: / we are all the work of your hands. / Be not so very angry, Lord, / keep not our guilt forever in mind; / look upon us, who are all your people. (Is 64:7-8)

**Rich in Clemency.** "I knew that you are a gracious and merciful God, slow to anger, rich in clemency, loathe to punish." (Jon 4:2c)

**Forsake Me Not.** *O Lord, in your anger punish me not, / in your wrath chastise me not;* / For your arrows have sunk deep in me, / and your hand has come down upon me. / There is no health in my flesh because of your indignation; / there is no wholeness in my bones because of my sin, / For my iniquities have overwhelmed me; / they are like a heavy burden, beyond my strength. / Noisome and festering are my sores / because of my folly, /I am stooped and bowed down profoundly; / all the day I go in mourning, / For my loins are filled with burning pains; / there is no health in my flesh. / I am numbed and severely crushed; / I roar with anguish of heart. / *O Lord, all my desire is before you; / from you my groaning is not hid.* /

My heart throbs; my strength forsakes me; / the very light of my eyes has failed me. / My friends and my companions stand back because of my affliction; / my neighbors stand afar off. / Men lay snares for me seeking my life; / they look to my misfortune, they speak of ruin, / treachery they talk of all the day. / But I am like a deaf man, hearing not, / like a dumb man who opens not his mouth. / I am become like a man who neither hears / nor has in his mouth a retort. / Because for you, O Lord, I wait; / you, O Lord my God, will answer / When I say, "Let them not be glad on my account / who, when my foot slips, glory over me." / For I am very near to falling, / and my grief is with me always. / Indeed, I acknowledge my guilt; / I grieve over my sin. / But my undeserved enemies are strong; / many are my foes without cause. / Those who repay evil for good / harass me for pursuing good. / *Forsake me not, O Lord; / my God, be not far from me! / Make haste to help me, / O Lord my salvation!* (Ps 38)

**God of Compassion.** *I have waited, waited for the Lord, / and he stooped toward me and heard my cry.* / He drew me out of the pit of destruction, / out of the mud of the swamp; / He set my feet upon a crag; / he made firm my steps. / And he put a new song into my mouth, / a hymn to our God. / Many shall look on in awe / and trust in the Lord. / Happy the man who makes the Lord his trust; / who turns not to idolatry / or to those who stray after falsehood. / How numerous have you made, / O Lord, my God, your wondrous deeds! / And in your plans for us / there is none to equal you; / Should I wish to declare or to tell them, / they would be too many to recount. /

Sacrifice or oblation you wished not, / but ears open to obedience you gave me. / Holocausts or sin-offerings you sought not; / then said I, "Behold I come; / in the written scroll it is prescribed for me. / To do your will, O my God, is my delight, / and your law is within my heart!" / I announced your justice in the vast assembly; / I did not restrain my lips, as you, O Lord, know. / Your justice I kept not hid within my heart; / your faithfulness and your salvation I have spoken of; / I have made no secret of your kindness and your truth / in the vast assembly. / *Withhold not, O Lord, your compassion from me; / may your kindness and your truth ever preserve me.* / For all about me are evils beyond reckoning; / my sins so overcome me that I cannot see; / They are more numerous than the hairs of my head, / and my heart fails me. / Deign, O Lord, rescue me; / O Lord, make haste to help me. / Let all be put to shame and confusion who seek to snatch away my life. / Let them be turned back in disgrace / who desire my ruin. / Let them be dismayed in their shame / who say to me, "Aha, aha!" / But may all who seek you / exult and be glad in you, / And may those who love your salvation / say ever, "The Lord be glorified." / Though I am afflicted and poor, / yet the Lord thinks of me. / You are my help and my deliverer; / O my God, hold not back! (Ps 40)

**Resplendent Powerful One.** God is renowned in Judah, / in Israel great is his name. / In Salem is his abode; / his dwelling is in Zion. / There he shattered the flashing shafts of the bow, / shield and sword, and weapons of war. / *Resplendent you came, O powerful One, / from the everlasting mountains.* / Despoiled are the stouthearted; /

they sleep their sleep; / the hands of all the mighty ones have failed. / At your rebuke, O God of Jacob, / chariots and steeds lay stilled. / You are terrible; and who can withstand you / for the fury of your anger? / *From heaven you made your intervention heard; / the earth feared and was silent / When God arose for judgment, / to save all the afflicted of the earth.* / For wrathful Edom shall glorify you, / and the survivors of Hamath shall keep your festivals. / Make vows to the Lord, your God, and fulfill them; / let all round about him bring gifts to the terrible Lord / Who checks the pride of princes, / who is terrible to the kings of the earth. (Ps 76)

## 9. To Beg the Lord's Forgiveness

Scripture reveals over and over again that even our sins may be turned to our advantage. In bringing before God their brokenness through sin, thus acknowledging their need for forgiveness, men and women of biblical times touched God's "weak side" as it were, "O happy fault." "It is I, I, who wipe out, for my own sake, your offenses; your sins I remember no more" (Is 43:25).

**I Have Sinned Grievously.** "I have sinned grievously in what I have done. But now, Lord, forgive the guilt of your servant, for I have been very foolish." (2 Sm 24:10)

**We Did Not Listen.** "Yours, O Lord, our God, are compassion and forgiveness! Yet we rebelled against you and paid no heed to your command, O Lord, our God.... You, O Lord, our God, are just in all that you have done, for we did not listen to your voice." (Dn 9:9-10a, 14b)

**Give Ear, O My God.** "Hear, therefore, O God, the prayer and petition of your servant. . . . Give ear, O my God, and listen. . . . When we present our petition before you, we rely not on our just deeds, but on your great mercy. O Lord, hear! O Lord, pardon! O Lord, be attentive and act without delay, for your own sake, O my God." (Dn 9:17-19)

**Delights in Clemency.** Who is there like you, the God who removes guilt / and pardons sin for the remnant of his inheritance; / Who does not persist in anger forever, / but delights rather in clemency, / And will again have compassion on us, / treading underfoot our guilt? / You will cast into the depths of the sea / all our sins; . . . / As you have sworn to our fathers / from days of old. (Mi 7:18-20)

**He Will Redeem.** *O Lord, hear my prayer, / and let my cry come to you. / Hide not your face from me / in the day of my distress. / Incline your ear to me; / in the day when I call, answer me speedily. /* For my days vanish like smoke, / and my bones burn like fire. / Withered and dried up like grass is my heart; / I forget to eat my bread. / Because of my insistent sighing / I am reduced to skin and bone. / I am like a desert owl; / I have become like an owl among the ruins. / I am sleepless, and I moan; / I am like a sparrow alone on the housetop. / All the day my enemies revile me; / in their rage against me they make a curse of me. / For I eat ashes like bread / and mingle my drink with tears, / Because of your fury and your wrath; / for you lifted me up only to cast me down. / My days are like a lengthening shadow, / and I wither like grass. / But you, O Lord, abide forever, / and your name through all generations. / You will arise and have mercy on Zion, / for it is time to pity her, / for the appointed time has come. / For her stones are dear to your servants, / and her dust moves them to pity. / And the nations shall revere your name, O Lord, / and all the kings of the earth your glory, / When the Lord has rebuilt Zion / and appeared in his glory; / When he has regarded the prayer of the destitute, / and not despised their prayer. / Let this be written for the generation to come, / and let his future creatures praise the Lord: / "The Lord looked down from his holy height, / from heaven he beheld the earth, / To hear the groaning of the prisoners, / to release those doomed to die"— / That the name of the Lord may be declared in Zion; / and his praise, in Jerusalem, / When the peoples gather together, / and the kingdoms, to serve the Lord. / He has broken down my strength in the way; / he has cut short my days. / I say: O my God, / Take me not hence in the midst of my days; / through all generations your years endure. / Of old you established the earth, / and the heavens are the work of your hands. / They shall perish, but you remain / though all of them grow old like a garment. / Like clothing you change them, and they are changed, / but you are the same, and your years have no end. / The children of your servants shall abide, / and their posterity shall continue in your presence. (Ps 102)

**From the Depths.** *Out of the depths I cry to you, O Lord; / Lord, hear my voice! /* Let your ears be attentive / to my voice in supplication: / *If you, O Lord, mark iniquities, / Lord, who can stand? / But with you is forgiveness, / that you may be revered.* / I trust in the Lord; / my soul trusts in his word. / My soul waits for the Lord / more than sentinels wait for the dawn. / More than sentinels wait for the dawn, / let Israel wait for the Lord, / For with the Lord is kindness / *and with him is plenteous redemption;* / And he will redeem Israel / from all their iniquities. (Ps 130)

## 10. To Seek His Healing

Our sinfulness is often only the symptom of some area of our lives where we need the Lord's healing. In his tender love the Lord wants to heal the hurts, bitterness, resentments, worries, and anxieties that plague us throughout life. He reminds us, "I, the Lord, am your healer" (Ex 15:26). He is disappointed when we do not come to him for healing: "They did not know that I was their healer" (Hos 11:4).

**Please Heal.** "Please, not this! Pray, heal her!" (Nm 12:13)

**Faith Heals.** You rebuke offenders little by little, / warn them, and remind them of the sins they are committing, / that they may abandon their wickedness and believe in you, O Lord! (Wis 12:2)

**Only He Can Heal.** Why have you struck us a blow / that cannot be healed? / We wait for peace, to no avail; /

for a time of healing, but terror comes instead. / We recognize, O Lord, our wickedness, / the guilt of our fathers; / that we have sinned against you. / For your name's sake spurn us not, / disgrace not the throne of your glory; / remember your covenant with us, and break it not. (Jer 14:19b-21)

**I Am Not Worthy.** "I am not worthy to have you under my roof. Just give an order and my boy will get better." (Mt 8:8)

**You Can Cure Me.** "Lord, if you will to do so, you can cure me." (Lk 5:12)

**Have Pity on Us.** "Jesus, Master, have pity on us." (Lk 17:13)

**Cry for Healing.** O Lord, reprove me not in your anger, / nor chastise me in your wrath. / *Have pity on me, O Lord, for I am languishing; / heal me, O Lord, for my body is in terror; / My soul, too, is utterly terrified; / but you, O Lord, how long . . . ? / Return, O Lord, save my life; / rescue me because of your kindness,* / For among the dead no one remembers you; / in the nether world who gives you thanks? / I am wearied with sighing; / every night I flood my bed with weeping; / I drench my couch with my tears. / My eyes are dimmed with sorrow; / they have aged because of all my foes. / Depart from me, all evildoers, / for the Lord has heard the sound of my weeping; / The Lord has heard my plea; / the Lord has accepted my prayer. / All my enemies shall be put to shame in utter terror; / they shall fall back in sudden shame. (Ps 6)

**Divine Healer.** Happy is he who has regard for the lowly and the poor; / in the day of misfortune the Lord will deliver him. / The Lord will keep and preserve him; / he will make him happy on the earth, / and not give him over to the will of his enemies. / *The Lord will help him on his sickbed, / he will take away all his ailment when he is ill. / Once I said, "O Lord, have pity on me; / heal me, though I have sinned against you.* / My enemies say the worst of me: / 'When will he die and his name perish?' / When one comes to see me, he speaks without sincerity; / his heart stores up malice; / when he leaves he gives voice to it outside. / All my foes whisper together against me; / against me they imagine the worst: / 'A malignant disease fills his frame'; / and 'Now that he lies ill, he will not rise again.' / Even my friend who had my trust / and partook of my bread, has raised his heel against me. / But you, O Lord, have pity on me, and raise me up, / that I may repay them." / That you love me I know by this, / that my enemy does not triumph over me, / But because of my integrity you sustain me / and let me stand before you forever. / Blessed be the Lord, the God of Israel, / from all eternity and forever. Amen. Amen. (Ps 41)

**Heals Our Frailty.** Bless the Lord, O my soul; / and all my being, bless his holy name. / Bless the Lord, O my soul, / and forget not all his benefits; / *He pardons all your iniquities, / he heals all your ills. / He redeems your life from destruction, / he crowns you with kindness and compassion, / He fills your lifetime with good; / your youth is renewed like the eagle's.* / The Lord secures justice / and the rights of all the oppressed. / He has made known his ways to Moses, / and his deeds to the children of Israel. /

Merciful and gracious is the Lord, / slow to anger and abounding in kindness. / He will not always chide, / nor does he keep his wrath forever. / Not according to our sins does he deal with us, / nor does he requite us according to our crimes. / For as the heavens are high above the earth, / so surpassing is his kindness toward those who fear him. / As far as the east is from the west, / so far has he put our transgressions from us. / *As a father has compassion on his children, / so the Lord has compassion on those who fear him,* / For he knows how we are formed; / he remembers that we are dust. / Man's days are like those of grass; / like a flower of the field he blooms; / The wind sweeps over him and he is gone, / and his place knows him no more. / But the kindness of the Lord is from eternity / to eternity toward those who fear him, / And his justice toward children's children / among those who keep his covenant / and remember to fulfill his precepts. / The Lord has established his throne in heaven, / and his kingdom rules over all. / Bless the Lord, all you his angels, / you mighty in strength, who do his bidding, / obeying his spoken word. / Bless the Lord, all you his hosts, / his ministers, who do his will. / Bless the Lord, all his works, / everywhere in his domain. / Bless the Lord, O my soul! (Ps 103)

## 11. To Recall God's Fidelity

Friends, even family, may fail us in time of need, even reject or ostracize us, yet we are the adopted daughters and sons of a loving Father who is always faithful—a lover who will never go back on his word. How reassuringly he tells us, "Can a mother forget her infant, / be without tenderness for the child of her womb? / Even should she forget, / I will never forget you" (Is 49:15).

**No God but You.** "Great are you, Lord God! There is none like you and there is no God but you, just as we have heard it told. . . . And now, Lord God, you are God and your words are truth." (2 Sm 7:22, 28)

**Blessed Be My Rock.** "The Lord live! And blessed be my Rock! / Extolled be my God, rock of my salvation." (2 Sm 22:47)

**Covenant of Kindness.** "Lord, God of Israel, there is no God like you in heaven above or on earth below; you keep your covenant of kindness with your servants who are faithful to you with their whole heart. . . . You who spoke that promise, have this day, by your own power, brought it to fulfillment." (1 Kgs 8:23-24)

**Generous Promise.** "Blessed be the Lord who has given rest to his people Israel, just as he promised. Not a single word has gone unfulfilled of the entire generous promise he made. . . . May the Lord, our God, be with us as he was with our fathers and may he not forsake us nor cast us off. May he draw our hearts to himself, that we may follow him in everything and keep the commands, statutes, and ordinances which he enjoined on our fathers." (1 Kgs 8:56-58)

**Promises Fulfilled.** "These promises of yours you fulfilled, for you are just. . . . Now, therefore, O our God, great, mighty, and awesome God, you who in your mercy preserve the covenant, take into account all the disasters that have befallen us." (Neh 9:8b, 32)

**An Unfailing Stance.** For every way, O Lord! you magnified and glorified your people; / unfailing, you stood by them in every time and circumstance. (Wis 19:22)

**Ever Faithful.** Give thanks to the Lord, invoke his name; / make known among the nations his deeds. / Sing to him, sing his praise, / proclaim all his wondrous deeds. / Glory in his holy name; / rejoice, O hearts that seek the Lord! / Look to the Lord in his strength; / seek to serve him constantly. / *Recall the wondrous deeds that he has wrought, / his portents, and the judgments he has uttered,* / You descendants of Abraham, his servants, / sons of Jacob, his chosen ones! / He, the Lord, is our God; / throughout the earth his judgments prevail. / *He remembers forever his covenant / which he made binding for a thousand generations—* / Which he entered into with Abraham / and by his oath to Isaac; / Which he established for Jacob by statute, / for Israel as an everlasting covenant, / Saying, "To you will I give the land of Canaan / as your allotted inheritance." / When they were few in number, / a handful, and strangers there, / Wandering from nation to nation / and from one kingdom to another people, / He let no man oppress them, / and for their sake he rebuked kings: / "Touch not my anointed, / and to my prophets do no harm." / When he called down a famine on the land / and ruined the crop that sustained them, / He sent a man before them, / Joseph, sold as a slave; / They had weighed him down with fetters, / and he was bound with chains, / Till his prediction came to pass / and the word of the Lord proved him true. / The king sent and released him, / the ruler of the peoples set him free. / He made him lord of his house / and ruler of all his possessions, / that he might train his princes to be like him / and teach his elders wisdom. / Then Israel came to Egypt, / and Jacob sojourned in the land of Ham. / He greatly increased his people / and made them stronger than their foes, / Whose hearts he changed, so that they hated his people, / and dealt deceitfully with his servants. / He sent Moses his servant; / Aaron, whom he had chosen. / They wrought his signs among them, / and wonders in the land of Ham. / He sent the darkness; it grew dark, / but they rebelled against his words. / He turned their waters into blood / and killed their fish. / Their land swarmed with frogs, / even in the chambers of their kings. / He spoke, and there came swarms of flies; / gnats, throughout all their borders. / For rain he gave them hail, / with flashing fires throughout their land. / He struck down their vines and their fig trees / and shattered the trees throughout their borders. / He spoke, and there came locusts / and grasshoppers without number; / And they devoured every plant throughout the land; / they devoured the fruit of their soil. / Then he struck every first-born throughout their land, / the first fruits of all their manhood. / And he led them forth laden with silver and gold, / with not a weakling among their tribes. / Egypt rejoiced at their going, / for the dread of them had fallen upon it. / He spread a cloud to cover them / and fire to give them light by night. / *They asked, and he brought them quail, / and with bread from heaven he satisfied them.* / He cleft the rock, and the water gushed forth; / it flowed through the dry lands like a stream, / For he remembered his holy word / to his servant Abraham. / And he led forth his people with joy; / with shouts of joy, his chosen ones. / And he gave them the lands of the nations, / and they took what the peoples had toiled for, / That they might keep his statutes and observe his laws. Alleluia. (Ps 105)

**God's Wonders.** When Israel came forth from Egypt, / the house of Jacob from a people of alien tongue, / Judah became his sanctuary, / Israel his domain. / The sea beheld and fled; / Jordan turned back. / The mountains skipped like rams, / the hills like the lambs of the flock. / Why is it, O sea, that you flee? / O Jordan, that you turn back? / You mountains, that you skip like rams? / You hills, like the lambs of the flock? / *Before the face of the Lord, tremble, O earth, / before the face of the God of Jacob, / Who turned the rock into pools of water, / the flint into flowing springs.* (Ps 114)

**Solemn Promise.** Remember, O Lord, for David / all his anxious care: / How he swore to the Lord, / vowed to the Mighty One of Jacob: / "I will not enter the house I live in, / nor lie on the couch where I sleep; / I will give my eyes no sleep / my eyelids no rest, / Till I find a place for the Lord, / a dwelling for the Mighty One of Jacob." / Behold, we heard of it in Ephrathah; / we found it in the fields of Jaar. / Let us enter into his dwelling, / let us worship at his footstool. / Advance, O Lord, to your resting place / you and the ark of your majesty. / May your priests be clothed with justice; / let your faithful ones shout merrily for joy. / For the sake of David your servant, / reject not the plea of your anointed. / *The Lord swore to David / a firm promise from which he will not* withdraw: / *"Your own offspring / I will set upon your throne; /* If your sons keep my covenant / and the decrees which I shall teach them, / Their sons, too, forever / shall sit upon your throne." / For the Lord has chosen Zion; / he prefers her for his dwelling. / "Zion is my resting place forever; / in her will I dwell, for I prefer her. / I will bless her with abundant provision, / her poor I will fill with bread. / Her priests I will clothe with salvation, / and her faithful ones shall shout merrily for joy. / *In her will I make a horn to sprout forth for David; / I will place a lamp for my anointed.* / His enemies I will clothe with shame, / but upon him my crown shall shine." (Ps 132)

## 12. To Strengthen Our Faith

How exciting and reassuring is God's promise made in his word: "You will receive all that you pray for, provided you have faith" (Mt 21:22). "Faith is confident assurance concerning what we hope for, and conviction about things we do not see" (Heb 11:1). "It is owing to his favor that salvation is yours through faith. This is not your own doing, it is God's gift" (Eph 2:8).

**Canticle of Faith.** For though the fig tree blossom not / nor fruit be on the vines, / Though the yield of the olive fail / and the terraces produce no nourishment, / Though the flocks disappear from the fold / and there be no herd in the stalls, / Yet will I rejoice in the Lord / and exult in my saving God. / God, my Lord, is my strength; / he makes my feet swift as those of hinds / and enables me to go upon the heights. (Hb 3:17-19)

**No Doubt about It.** "Beyond doubt you are the Son of God!" (Mt 14:33)

**The Messiah.** "You are the Messiah, the Son of the living God!" (Mt 16:16)

**Act of Faith.** "My Lord and my God!" (Jn 20:28)

**Save Me.** O Lord, how many are my adversaries! / Many rise up against me! / Many are saying of me, / "There is no salvation for him in God." / *But you, O Lord, are my shield; / my glory, you lift up my head! / When I call out to the Lord, / he answers me from his holy mountain. / When I lie down in sleep, / I wake again for the Lord sustains me.* / I fear not the myriads of people / arrayed against me on every side. / Rise up, O Lord! / Save me, my God! / For you strike all my enemies on the cheek; / the teeth of the wicked you break. / Salvation is the Lord's! / Upon your people be your blessing! (Ps 3)

**My Heart Exults.** To you, O Lord, I call; / O my Rock be not deaf to me, / Lest, if you heed me not, / I become one of those going down into the pit. / Hear the sound of my pleading, when I cry to you, / lifting up my hands toward your holy shrine. / Drag me not away with the wicked, / with those who do wrong, / Who speak civilly to their neighbors / though evil is in their hearts. / Repay them for their deeds, / for the evil of their doings. / For the work of their hands repay them; / give them their deserts. / Because they consider not / the deeds of the Lord nor the work of his hands, / may he tear them down and not build them up. / *Blessed be the Lord, / for he has* *heard the sound of my pleading; / the Lord is my strength and my shield. / In him my heart trusts, and I find help; / then my heart exults, and with my song I give him thanks. /* The Lord is the strength of his people, / the saving refuge of his anointed. / Save your people, and bless your inheritance, / feed them, and carry them forever! (Ps 28)

**Be Glad in the Lord.** The Lord is king; let the earth rejoice; / let the many isles be glad. / Clouds and darkness are round about him, / justice and judgment are the foundation of his throne. / Fire goes before him / and consumes his foes round about. / His lightnings illumine the world; / the earth sees and trembles. / The mountains melt like wax before the Lord, / before the Lord of all the earth. / The heavens proclaim his justice, / and all peoples see his glory. / All who worship graven things are put to shame, / who glory in the things of nought; / all gods are prostrate before him. / Zion hears and is glad, / and the cities of Judah rejoice / because of your judgments, O Lord. / Because you, O Lord, are the Most High over all the earth, / exalted far above all gods. / *The Lord loves those that hate evil; / he guards the lives of his faithful ones; / from the hand of the wicked he delivers them. / Light dawns for the just; / and gladness, for the upright of heart. / Be glad in the Lord, you just, / and give thanks to his holy name.* (Ps 97)

## 13. To Fortify Our Hope

Christian hope differs from our ordinary understanding of the word *hope*. Christian hope arises from our experience of God as a Father who loves us with an infinite love and who is always faithful to his promises. It is a desire, a yearning, to reach a state of perfect happiness with him. St. Paul prays, "May God, the source of hope, fill you with all joy and peace in believing so that through the power of the Holy Spirit you may have hope in abundance" (Rom 15:13).

**Only the Lord.** What a wretched man I am! Who can free me from this body under the power of death? All praise to God, through Jesus Christ our Lord! (Rom 7:24-25a)

**Hope Eternal.** May our Lord Jesus Christ himself, may God our Father who loved us and in his mercy gave us eternal consolation and hope, console your hearts and strengthen them for every good work and word. (2 Thes 2:16-17)

**A New Birth.** Praised be the God and Father / of our Lord Jesus Christ, / he who in his great mercy / gave us new birth; / a birth unto hope which draws its life / from the resurrection of Jesus Christ from the dead; / a birth to an imperishable inheritance, / incapable of fading or defilement, / which is kept in heaven for you / who are guarded with God's power through faith; / a birth to a salvation which stands ready / to be revealed in the last days. (1 Pt 1:3-5)

**Justice Prevails.** *Do me justice, O Lord! for I have walked in integrity, / and in the Lord I trust without wavering. / Search me, O Lord, and try me; / test my soul and my heart. / For* your kindness is before my eyes, / and I walk in your truth. / I stay not with worthless men, / nor do I consort with hypocrites. / I hate the assembly of evildoers, / and with the wicked I will not stay. / I wash my hands in innocence, / and I go around your altar, O Lord, / Giving voice to my thanks, / and recounting all your wondrous deeds. / O Lord, I love the house in which you dwell, / the tenting-place of your glory. / Gather not my soul with those of sinners, / nor with men of blood my life. / On their hands are crimes, / and their right hands are full of bribes. / But I walk in integrity; / redeem me, and have pity on me. / My foot stands on level ground; / in the assemblies I will bless the Lord. (Ps 26)

**Hope in Abundance.** May God, the source of hope, fill you with all joy and peace in believing so that through the power of the Holy Spirit you may have hope in abundance. (Rom 15:13)

**Hope in God.** Do me justice, O God, and fight my fight / against a faithless people; / from the deceitful and impious man rescue me. / For you, O God, are my strength. / Why do you keep me so far away? / Why must I go about in mourning, / with the enemy oppressing me? / *Send forth your light and your fidelity; / they shall lead me on / And bring me to your holy mountain, / to your dwelling-place. /* Then will I go in to the altar of God, / the God of my gladness and joy; / Then will I give you thanks upon the harp, / O God, my God! / *Why are you so downcast, O my soul? / Why do you sigh within me? / Hope in God! For I shall again be thanking him, / in the presence of my savior and my God.* (Ps 43)

**When Threatened.** Hear, O God, my voice in my lament; / from the dread enemy preserve my life. / Shelter me against the council of malefactors, / against the tumult of evildoers, / Who sharpen their tongues like swords, / who aim like arrows their bitter words, / Shooting from ambush at the innocent man, / suddenly shooting at him without fear. / They resolve on their wicked plan; / they conspire to set snares, / saying, "Who will see us?" / They devise a wicked scheme, / and conceal the scheme they have devised; / deep are the thoughts of each heart. / But God shoots his arrows at them; / suddenly they are struck. / He brings them down by their own tongues; / all who see them nod their heads. / And all men fear and proclaim the work of God, / and ponder what he has done. / *The just man is glad in the Lord and takes refuge in him; / in him glory all the upright of heart.* (Ps 64)

**Firm Hope.** Praise the Lord, O my soul; / I will praise the Lord all my life; / I will sing praise to my God while I live. / *Put not your trust in princes, / in man, in whom there is no salvation.* / When his spirit departs he returns to his earth; / on that day his plans perish. / *Happy he whose help is the God of Jacob, / whose hope is in the Lord, his God, / Who made heaven and earth, / the sea and all that is in them; / Who keeps faith forever,* / secures justice for the oppressed, / gives food to the hungry. / The Lord sets captives free; / the Lord gives sight to the blind. / The Lord raises up those that were bowed down; / the Lord loves the just. / The Lord protects strangers; / the fatherless and the widow he sustains, / but the way of the wicked he thwarts. / The Lord shall reign forever; / your God, O Zion, through all generations. Alleluia. (Ps 146)

## 14. *To Preserve Our Trust*

If we are honest with ourselves, we must admit that it is difficult for us to trust God implicitly. It is easier for us to trust others, since they know our human limitations and will not ask too much of us, but we are not certain if God will ask more than we are willing to give. "Trust in the Lord with all your heart, / on your own intelligence rely not; / In all your ways be mindful of him, / and he will make straight your paths" (Prv 3:5-6).

**Lord, Be Attentive.** "O Lord, God of heaven, great and awesome God, you who preserve your covenant of mercy toward those who love you and keep your commandments, may your ear be attentive, and your eyes open, to heed the prayer which I, your servant, now offer in your presence day and night for your servants . . . confessing the sins which we . . . have committed against you, I and my father's house included. Grievously have we offended you, not keeping the commandments. . . . O Lord, may your ear be attentive to my prayer and that of all your willing servants who revere your name. Grant success to your servant this day." (Neh 1:5-7a, 11)

**No God but You.** Come to our aid, O God of the universe, / and put all the nations in dread of you! / Raise your hand against the heathen, / that they may realize your power. / As you have used us to show them your holiness, / so now use them to show us your glory. / Thus they will know, as we know, / that there is no God but you. / Give new signs and work new wonders; / show forth the splendor of your right hand and arm. (Sir 36:1-5)

**Trust in the Lord.** "A nation of firm purpose you keep in peace; / in peace, for its trust in you." / Trust in the Lord forever! / For the Lord is an eternal Rock. (Is 26:3-4)

**Total Gift.** "Father, into your hands I commend my spirit." (Lk 23:46)

**Sleep Peacefully.** When I call, answer me, O my just God, / you who relieve me when I am in distress; / Have pity on me, and hear my prayer! / Men of rank, how long will you be dull of heart? / Why do you love what is vain and seek after falsehood? / *Know that the Lord does wonders for his faithful one; / the Lord will hear me when I call upon him. / Tremble, and sin not; / reflect, upon your beds, in silence. / Offer just sacrifices, and trust in the Lord.* / Many say, "Oh, that we might see better times!" / O Lord, let the light of your countenance shine upon us! / You put gladness into my heart, / more than when grain and wine abound. / As soon as I lie down, I fall peacefully asleep, / for you alone, O Lord, / bring security to my dwelling. (Ps 4)

**In Adversity.** *In the Lord I take refuge; how can you say to me, / "Flee to the mountain like a bird!* / For, see, the wicked bend the bow; / they place the arrow on the string / to shoot in the dark at the upright of heart. / When the pillars are overthrown, / what can the just man do?" / The Lord is in his holy temple; / the Lord's throne is in heaven. / His eyes behold, / his searching glance is on mankind. / The Lord searches the just and the wicked; / the love of violence he hates. / He rains upon the wicked fiery coals and brimstone; / a burning blast is their allotted cup. / *For the Lord is just, he loves just deeds; / the upright shall see his face.* (Ps 11)

**Unbounded Confidence.** Have pity on me, O God, for men trample upon me; / all the day they press their attack against me. / My adversaries trample upon me all the day; / yes, many fight against me. / O Most High, when I begin to fear, / in you will I trust. / In God, in whose promise I glory, / in God I trust without fear; / what can flesh do against me? / All the day they molest me in my efforts; / their every thought is of evil against me. / They gather together in hiding, / they watch my steps. / As they have waited for my life, / because of their wickedness keep them in view: / in your wrath bring down the peoples, O God. / My wanderings you have counted; / my tears are stored in your flask; / are they not recorded in your book? / Then do my enemies turn back, / when I call upon you; / now I know that God is with me. / *In God, in whose promise I glory, / in God I trust without fear; / what can flesh do against me?* / I am bound, O God, by vows to you; / your thank offerings I will fulfill. / For you have rescued me from death, / my feet, too, from stumbling; / that I may walk before God in the light of the living. (Ps 56)

**Troubled Times.** Only in God is my soul at rest; / from him comes my salvation. / He only is my rock and my salvation, / my stronghold; I shall not be disturbed at all. / How long will you set upon a man and all together beat him down / as though he were a sagging fence, a battered wall? / Truly from my place on high they plan to dislodge me; / they delight in lies; / They bless with their mouths, / but inwardly they curse. / *Only in God be at rest, my soul, / for from him comes my hope. / He only is my rock and my salvation, / my stronghold; I shall not be disturbed. / With God is my safety and my glory, / he is the rock of my strength; /*

*my refuge is in God. / Trust in him at all times, O my people! /
Pour out your hearts before him; / God is our refuge! /* Only a
breath are mortal men; / an illusion are men of rank; / In
a balance they prove lighter, / all together, than a breath.
/ Trust not in extortion; in plunder take no empty pride;
/ though wealth abound, set not your heart upon it. /
One thing God said; these two things which I heard: /
that power belongs to God, and yours, / O Lord, is
kindness; / and that you render to everyone according to
his deeds. (Ps 62)

**Under Siege.** Deliver me, O Lord, from evil men; /
preserve me from violent men, / From those who devise
evil in their hearts, / and stir up wars every day. / They
make their tongues sharp as those of serpents; / the
venom of asps is under their lips. / Save me, O Lord,
from the hands of the wicked; / preserve me from violent
men / Who plan to trip up my feet— / the proud who
have hidden a trap for me; / They have spread cords for a
net; / by the wayside they have laid snares for me. / I say
to the Lord, you are my God; / hearken, O Lord, to my
voice in supplication. / O God, my Lord, my strength
and my salvation; / you are my helmet in the day of battle!
/ Grant not, O Lord, the desires of the wicked; / further
not their plans. / Those who surround me lift up their
heads; / may the mischief which they threaten overwhelm
them. / May he rain burning coals upon them; / may he
cast them into the depths, never to rise. / A man of
wicked tongue shall not abide in the land; / evil shall
abruptly entrap the violent man. / *I know that the Lord
renders / justice to the afflicted, judgment to the poor. / Surely
the just shall give thanks to your name: / the upright shall
dwell in your presence.* (Ps 140)

## *15. To Enrich Our Love*

Do you ever wonder if God really loves you, with all your little infidelities, weaknesses, self-centeredness? Throughout his word the Lord tells us that he loves us just as we are, with all our shortcomings, faults, and failings. Jesus spelled it out plainly, "As the Father has loved me, so I have loved you. Live on in my love" (Jn 15:9).

**You Know Well.** "Lord, you know everything. You know well that I love you." (Jn 21:17b)

**Unfailing Love.** Grace be with all who love our Lord Jesus Christ with unfailing love. (Eph 6:24)

**Rich Harvest.** My prayer is that your love may more and more abound, both in understanding and wealth of experience, so that with a clear conscience and blameless conduct you may learn to value the things that really matter, up to the very day of Christ. It is my wish that you may be found rich in the harvest of justice which Jesus Christ has ripened in you, to the glory and praise of God. (Phil 1:9-11)

**Overflow with Love.** May God himself, who is our Father, and our Lord Jesus make our path to you a straight one! And may the Lord increase you and make you overflow with love for one another and for all, even as our love does for you. May he strengthen your hearts, making them blameless and holy before our God and Father at the coming of our Lord Jesus with all his holy ones. (1 Thes 3:11-13)

**I Love You, Lord.** *I love you, O Lord, my strength, / O Lord, my rock, my fortress, my deliverer. / My God, my rock of refuge, / my shield, the horn of my salvation, my stronghold! /* Praised be the Lord, I exclaim, / and I am safe from my enemies. / The breakers of death surged round about me, / the destroying floods overwhelmed me; / The cords of the nether world enmeshed me, / the snares of death overtook me. / In my distress I called upon the Lord / and cried out to my God; / From his temple he heard my voice, / and my cry to him reached his ears. / The earth swayed and quaked; / the foundations of the mountains trembled / and shook when his wrath flared up. / Smoke rose from his nostrils, / and a devouring fire from his mouth / that kindled coals into flame. / And he inclined the heavens and came down, / with dark clouds under his feet. / He mounted a cherub and flew, / borne on the wings of the wind. / And he made darkness the cloak about him; / dark, misty rain-clouds his wrap. / From the brightness of his presence / coals were kindled to flame. / And the Lord thundered from heaven, / the Most High gave forth his voice; / He sent forth his arrows to put them to flight, / with frequent lightnings he routed them. / Then the bed of the sea appeared, / and the foundations of the world were laid bare, / At the rebuke of the Lord, / at the blast of the wind of his wrath. / He reached out from on high and grasped me; / he drew me out of the deep waters. / He rescued me from my mighty enemy / and from my foes, who were too powerful for me. / They attacked me in the day of my calamity, / but the Lord came to my support. / He set me free in the open, / and rescued me, because he loves me. / The Lord rewarded me according to justice; / according to the cleanness of my hands he requited me; / for I kept the ways of the Lord and was not disloyal to my God; / For his ordinances were all present to me, / and his statutes I put not from me, / But I was wholehearted toward him, / and I was on my guard against guilt. / And the Lord requited me according to my justice, / according to the cleanness of my hands in his sight. / *Toward the faithful you are faithful, / toward the wholehearted you are wholehearted,* / Toward the sincere you are sincere, / but toward the crooked you are astute; / For lowly people you save / but haughty eyes you bring low; / *You indeed, O Lord, give light to my lamp; / O my God, you brighten the darkness about me;* / For with your aid I run against an armed band, / and by the help of my God I leap over a wall. / God's way is unerring, / the promise of the Lord is fire-tried; / he is a shield to all who take refuge in him. / For who is God except the Lord? / Who is a rock, save our God? / The God who girded me with strength / and kept my way unerring; / Who made my feet swift as those of hinds / and set me on the heights; / Who trained my hands for war / and my arms to bend a bow of brass. / You have given me your saving shield; / your right hand has upheld me, / and you have stooped to make me great. / You made room for my steps; / unwavering was my stride. / I pursued my enemies and overtook them, / nor did I turn again till I made an end of them. / I smote them and they could not rise; / they fell beneath my feet. / And you girded me with strength for war; / you subdued my adversaries beneath me. / My enemies you put to flight before me, / and those who hated me you destroyed. / They cried for help—but no one saved them; / to the Lord—but he answered them not. / I ground them fine as the dust before the wind; / like the mud in the streets I trampled them down. / You rescued me from the strife of the people, / you made me head over nations; / A people I had not known became my slaves; / as soon as they heard me they obeyed. / The foreigners fawned and cringed before me, / they staggered forth from their fortresses. / The Lord live! And blessed be my Rock! / Extolled be God my savior. / O God, who granted me vengeance, / who made peoples subject to me / and preserved me from my enemies, / Truly above my adversaries you exalt me / and from the violent man you have rescued me. / Therefore will I proclaim you, O Lord, among the nations, / and I will sing praise to your name, / You who gave great victories to your king / and showed kindness to your anointed, / to David and his posterity forever. (Ps 18)

**Love the Lord.** In you, O Lord, I take refuge, / let me never be put to shame. / In your justice rescue me, / incline your ear to me, / make haste to deliver me! / Be my rock of refuge, / a stronghold to give me safety. / You are my rock and my fortress; / for your name's sake you will lead and guide me. / You will free me from the snare they set for me, / for you are my refuge. / *Into your hands I commend my spirit; / you will redeem me, O Lord, O faithful God.* / You hate those who worship vain idols, / but my trust is in the Lord. / I will rejoice and be glad of your kindness, / when you have seen my affliction / and watched over me in my distress, / Not shutting me up in the grip of the enemy / but enabling me to move about at large. / Have pity on me, O Lord, for I am in distress; / with sorrow my eye is consumed; my soul also, and my body. / For my life is spent with grief / and my years with sighing; / My strength has failed through affliction, / and my bones are consumed. / For all my foes I am an object of reproach, / a laughingstock to my neighbors, and a dread to my friends; / they who see me abroad flee from me. / I am forgotten like the unremembered dead; / I am like a dish that is broken. / I hear the whispers of the crowd, that frighten me from every side, / as they consult together against me, plotting to take my life. / *But my trust is in you, O Lord; / I say, "You are my God." /* In your hands is my destiny; rescue me / from the clutches of my enemies and my persecutors. / Let your face shine upon your servant; / save me in your kindness. / O Lord, let me not be put to shame, for I call upon you; / let the wicked be put to shame; let them be reduced to silence in the nether world. / Let dumbness strike their lying lips / that speak insolence against the just in pride and scorn. / How great is the goodness, O Lord, / which you have in store for those who fear you, / And which, toward those who take refuge in you, / you show in the sight of men. / You hide them in the shelter of your presence / from the plottings of men; / You screen them within your abode / from the strife of tongues. / Blessed be the Lord whose wondrous kindness / he has shown me in a fortified city. / Once I said in my anguish, / "I am cut off from your sight"; / Yet you heard the sound of my pleading / when I cried out to you. / *Love the Lord, all you his faithful ones! / The Lord keeps those who are constant, / but more than requites those who act proudly. / Take courage and be stouthearted, / all you who hope in the Lord.* (Ps 31)

**A Name We Love.** Praise the name of the Lord; / Praise, you servants of the Lord / Who stand in the house of the Lord, / in the courts of the house of our God. / *Praise the Lord, for the Lord is good; / sing praise to his name, which we love; /* For the Lord has chosen Jacob for himself, / Israel for his own possession. / *For I know that the Lord is great; / our Lord is greater than all gods.* / All that the Lord wills he does / in heaven and on earth, / in the seas and in all the deeps. / He raises storm clouds from the end of the earth; / with the lightning he makes the rain; / he brings forth the winds from his storehouse. / He smote the first-born in Egypt, / both of man and of beast. / He sent signs and wonders / into your midst, O Egypt, / against Pharaoh and against all his servants. / He smote many nations / and slew mighty kings: / Sihon, king of the Amorites, / and Og, king of Bashan, / and all the kings of Canaan; / And he made their land a heritage, / the heritage of Israel his people. / Your name, O Lord, endures forever; / Lord is your title through all generations, / For the Lord defends his people, / and is merciful to his servants. / The idols of the nations are silver and gold, / the handiwork of men. / They have mouths but speak not; / they have eyes but see not; / They have ears but hear not, / nor is there breath in their mouths. / Their makers shall be like them, / everyone that trusts in them. / House of Israel, bless the Lord, / house of Aaron, bless the Lord, / House of Levi, bless the Lord; / you who fear the Lord, bless the Lord. / Blessed from Zion be the Lord, / who dwells in Jerusalem. (Ps 135)

## 16. To Increase Our Longing

St. Augustine said it so well: "Our hearts are restless until they rest in you." So many of the things in life are ephemeral, fleeting, empty. Only in the Lord can we find fulfillment. The more earnestly we long for him, the greater will be our joy. Jesus invites us, "Come to me, all you who are weary and find life burdensome, and I will refresh you" (Mt 11:28). And we respond, "Come, Lord Jesus!" (Rv 22:20).

**My Soul Yearns.** The way of the just is smooth; / the path of the just you make level. / Yes, for your way and your judgments, O Lord, / we look to you; / Your name and your title / are the desire of our souls. / My soul yearns for you in the night, / yes, my spirit within me keeps vigil for you. (Is 26:7-9a)

**We Come to You.** "Here we are, we now come to you / because you are the Lord, our God. / Deceptive indeed are the hills, / the thronging mountains; / In the Lord, our God, alone / is the salvation of Israel. . . .

Let us lie down in our shame, / let our disgrace cover us, / for we have sinned against the Lord, our God, / From our youth to this day, we and our fathers also; / we listened not to the voice of the Lord, our God." (Jer 3:22b-23, 25)

**Athirst Is My Soul.** *As the hind longs for the running waters, / so my soul longs for you, O God. / Athirst is my soul for God, the living God. / When shall I go and behold the face of God? / My tears are my food day and night, / as they say to me day after day, "Where is your God?" / Those times I recall, / now that I pour out my soul within me, / When I went with the throng / and led them in procession to the house of God, / Amid loud cries of joy and thanksgiving, / with the multitude keeping festival. / Why are you so downcast, O my soul? / Why do you sigh* within me? / Hope in God! For I shall again be thanking him, / in the presence of my savior and my God. / Within me my soul is downcast; / so will I remember you / From the land of the Jordan and of Hermon, / from Mount Mizar. / Deep calls unto deep / in the roar of your cataracts; / All your breakers and your billows / pass over me. / By day the Lord bestows his grace, / and at night I have his song, / a prayer to my living God. / I sing to God, my rock: / "Why do you forget me? / Why must I go about in mourning, / with the enemy oppressing me?" / It crushes my bones that my foes mock me, / as they say to me day after day, "Where is your God?" / Why are you so downcast, O my soul? / Why do you sigh within me? / *Hope in God! For I shall again be thanking him, / in the presence of my savior and my God.* (Ps 42)

**Ardent Longing.** *O God, you are my God whom I seek; / for you my flesh pines and my soul thirsts / like the earth, parched, lifeless and without water.* / Thus have I gazed toward you in the sanctuary / to see your power and your glory, / For your kindness is a greater good than life; / my lips shall glorify you. / Thus will I bless you while I live; / lifting up my hands, I will call upon your name. / As with the riches of a banquet shall my soul be satisfied, / and with exultant lips my mouth shall praise you. / *I will remember you upon my couch, / and through the night-watches I will meditate on you: / That you are my help, / and in the shadow of your wings I shout for joy. / My soul clings fast to you; / your right hand upholds me.* / But they shall be destroyed who seek my life, / they shall go into the depths of the earth; / They shall be delivered over to the sword, / and shall be the prey of jackals. / The king, however, shall rejoice in God; / everyone who swears by him shall glory, / but the mouths of those who speak falsely shall be stopped. (Ps 63)

**His Dwelling Place.** *How lovely is your dwelling place, / O Lord of hosts! / My soul yearns and pines / for the courts of the Lord. / My heart and my flesh / cry out for the living God. /* Even the sparrow finds a home, / and the swallow a nest / in which she puts her young— / Your altars, O Lord of hosts, / my king and my God! / Happy they who dwell in your house! / continually they praise you. / Happy the men whose strength you are! / their hearts are set upon the pilgrimage: / When they pass through the valley of the mastic trees / they make a spring of it; / the early rain clothes it with generous growth. / They go from strength to strength; / they shall see the God of gods in Zion. / O Lord of hosts, hear my prayer; / hearken, O God of Jacob! / O God, behold our shield, / and look upon the face of your anointed. / I had rather one day in your courts / than a thousand elsewhere; / I had rather lie at the threshold of the house of my God / than dwell in the tents of the wicked. / For a sun and a shield is the Lord God; / grace and glory he bestows; / The Lord withholds no good thing / from those who walk in sincerity. / O Lord of hosts, / happy the men who trust in you! (Ps 84)

**Home at Last.** *By the streams of Babylon / we sat and wept / when we remembered Zion. / On the aspens of that land / we hung up our harps, / Though there our captors asked of us / the*

*lyrics of our songs, / And our despoilers urged us to be joyous: /
"Sing for us the songs of Zion!"* / How could we sing a song
of the Lord / in a foreign land? / If I forget you,
Jerusalem, / may my right hand be forgotten! / May my
tongue cleave to my palate / if I remember you not, / If I
place not Jerusalem / ahead of my joy. / Remember, O
Lord, against the children of Edom, / the day of
Jerusalem, / When they said, "Raze it, raze it / down to
its foundations!" / O daughter of Babylon, you de-
stroyer, / happy the man who shall repay you / the evil
you have done us! / Happy the man who shall seize and
smash / your little ones against the rock! (Ps 137)

## 17. To Find Peace in His Presence

The Hebrew word *shalom* means much more than our
word *peace*. *Shalom* includes the sum total of all blessings,
particularly salvation. Since Jesus is our redeemer, he
could say, " 'Peace' is my farewell to you, my peace is my
gift to you" (Jn 14:27). And St. Paul reassures us, "It is he
who is our peace" (Eph 2:14a).

**Blessings of Peace.** The Lord bless you and keep you! /
The Lord let his face shine upon you, and / be gracious to
you! / The Lord look upon you kindly and give / you
peace! (Nm 6:24-26)

**You Mete Out Peace.** O Lord, you mete out peace to us,
/ for it is you who have accomplished all we have done. /
O Lord, our God, other lords than you have ruled us; / it
is from you only that we can call upon your name. (Is
26:12-13)

**Peace of God.** We wish you the favor and peace of God our Father and of the Lord Jesus Christ, who gave himself for our sins, to rescue us from the present evil age, as our God and Father willed—to him be glory for endless ages. Amen. (Gal 1:3-5)

**Peace and Mercy.** All that matters is that one is created anew. Peace and mercy on all who follow this rule of life. (Gal 6:15b-16a)

**All That Is Good.** May the God of peace, who brought up from the dead the great Shepherd of the sheep by the blood of the eternal covenant, Jesus our Lord, furnish you with all that is good, that you may do his will. Through Jesus Christ may he carry out in you all that is pleasing to him. To Christ be glory forever! Amen. (Heb 13:20-21)

**Holy Mountain.** *O Lord, who shall sojourn in your tent? / Who shall dwell on your holy mountain?* / He who walks blamelessly and does justice; / who thinks the truth in his heart / and slanders not with his tongue; / Who harms not his fellow man, / nor takes up a reproach against his neighbor; / By whom the reprobate is despised, / while he honors those who fear the Lord; / Who, though it be to his loss, changes not his pledged word; / who lends not his money at usury / and accepts no bribe against the innocent. / He who does these things / shall never be disturbed. (Ps 15)

**Sheltering Presence.** The Lord is my light and my salvation; / whom should I fear? / The Lord is my life's refuge; / of whom should I be afraid? / When evildoers

come at me / to devour my flesh, / My foes and my
enemies / themselves stumble and fall. / Though an army
encamp against me, / my heart will not fear; / Though
war be waged upon me, / even then will I trust. / *One
thing I ask of the Lord; / this I seek: / To dwell in the house of
the Lord / all the days of my life, / That I may gaze on the
loveliness of the Lord / and contemplate his temple. / For he
will hide me in his abode / in the day of trouble; / He will
conceal me in the shelter of his tent, / he will set me high upon a
rock.* / Even now my head is held high / above my
enemies on every side. / And I will offer in his tent /
sacrifices with shouts of gladness; / I will sing and chant
praise to the Lord. / Hear, O Lord, the sound of my call;
/ have pity on me, and answer me. / Of you my heart
speaks; you my glance seeks; / your presence, O Lord, I
seek. / Hide not your face from me; / do not in anger
repel your servant. / You are my helper: cast me not off; /
forsake me not, O God my savior. / Though my father
and mother forsake me, / yet will the Lord receive me. /
Show me, O Lord, your way, / and lead me on a level
path, / because of my adversaries. / Give me not up to the
wishes of my foes; / for false witnesses have risen up
against me, / and such as breathe out violence. / I believe
that I shall see the bounty of the Lord / in the land of the
living. / Wait for the Lord with courage; / be stouthearted, and wait for the Lord. (Ps 27)

**City of God.** His foundation upon the holy mountains /
the Lord loves: / The gates of Zion, / more than any
dwelling of Jacob. / *Glorious things are said of you, / O city
of God!* / I tell of Egypt and Babylon / among those that
know the Lord; / Of Philistia, Tyre, Ethiopia: / "This

man was born there." / And of Zion they shall say: / "One and all were born in her; / And he who has established her / is the Most High Lord." / They shall note, when the peoples are enrolled: / "This man was born there." / *And all shall sing, in their festive dance: / "My home is within you."* (Ps 87)

**Abiding Presence.** Not to us, O Lord, not to us / but to your name give glory / because of your kindness, because of your truth. / Why should the pagans say, / "Where is their God?" / *Our God is in heaven; / whatever he wills, he does.* / Their idols are silver and gold, / the handiwork of men. / They have mouths but speak not; / they have eyes but see not; / They have ears but hear not; / they have noses but smell not; / They have hands but feel not; / they have feet but walk not; / they utter no sound from their throat. / Their makers shall be like them, / everyone that trusts in them. / The house of Israel trusts in the Lord; / he is their help and their shield. / The house of Aaron trusts in the Lord; / he is their help and their shield. / *Those who fear the Lord trust in the Lord; / he is their help and their shield. / The Lord remembers us and will bless us:* / he will bless the house of Israel; / he will bless the house of Aaron; / He will bless those who fear the Lord, / both the small and the great. / May the Lord bless you more and more, / both you and your children. / May you be blessed by the Lord, / who made heaven and earth. / Heaven is the heaven of the Lord, / but the earth he has given to the children of men. / It is not the dead who praise the Lord, / nor those who go down into silence, / But we bless the Lord, / both now and forever. (Ps 115)

## *18. To Rest in Our Only Refuge*

On our journey through life en route to our final destiny, we can encounter many dangers, both physical and spiritual, lurking along the way. We can be eternally grateful that we have a divine rescuer who is delighted to respond to our call for help. "The Lord is good, / a refuge on the day of distress; / He takes care of those who have recourse to him" (Na 1:7).

**All Alone.** "My Lord, our King, you alone are God. Help me, who am alone and have no help but you. . . . Be mindful of us, O Lord. Manifest yourself in the time of our distress and give me courage. King of gods and Ruler of every power. . . . Save us by your power, and help me, who am alone and have no one but you, O Lord. . . . O God, more powerful than all, hear the voice of those in despair. Save us from the power of the wicked, and deliver me from my fear." (Est C:14, 23, 25, 30)

**Eternal God.** Hear the prayer of your servants, / for you are ever gracious to your people; / Thus it will be known to the very ends of the earth / that you are the eternal God. (Sir 36:16-17)

**Refuge to the Poor.** For you are a refuge to the poor, / a refuge to the needy in distress; / Shelter from the rain, / shade from the heat. (Is 25:4)

**Raise a Glad Cry.** Raise a glad cry, you heavens: the Lord has done this; / shout, you depths of the earth. / Break forth, you mountains, into song, / you forest, with all your trees. / For the Lord has redeemed Jacob, / and shows his glory through Israel. (Is 44:23)

**Your Holy Dwelling.** "Hear, O Lord, our prayer of supplication, and deliver us for your own sake: grant us favor in the presence of our captors, that the whole earth may know that you are the Lord, our God. . . . O Lord, look down from your holy dwelling and take thought of us; turn, O Lord, your ear to hear us." (Bar 2:14-16)

**Safe Rescue.** To you I lift up my soul, / O Lord, my God. / In you I trust; let me not be put to shame, / let not my enemies exult over me. / No one who waits for you shall be put to shame; / those shall be put to shame who heedlessly break faith. / Your ways, O Lord, make known to me; / teach me your paths, / Guide me in your truth and teach me, / for you are God my savior, / and for you I wait all the day. / Remember that your compassion, O Lord, / and your kindness are from of old. / The sins of my youth and my frailties remember not; / in your kindness remember me, / because of your goodness, O Lord. / Good and upright is the Lord; / thus he shows sinners the way. / He guides the humble to justice, / he teaches the humble his way. / *All the paths of the Lord are kindness and constancy / toward those who keep his covenant and his decrees.* / For your name's sake, O Lord, / you will pardon my guilt, great as it is. / When a man fears the Lord, / he shows him the way he should choose. / He abides in prosperity, / and his descendants inherit the land. / The friendship of the Lord is with those who fear him, / and his covenant, for their instruction. / My eyes are ever toward the Lord, / for he will free my feet from the snare. / Look toward me, and have pity on me, / for I am alone and afflicted. / Relieve the troubles of my heart, / and bring me out of my distress. / Put an end to my affliction and my suffering, / and take away all my sins. / Behold, my enemies are many, / and they hate me violently. / *Preserve my life, and rescue me; / let me not be put to shame, for I take refuge in you.* / Let integrity and uprightness preserve me, / because I wait for you, O Lord. / Redeem Israel, O God, / from all its distress! (Ps 25)

**Tower of Strength.** Hear, O God, my cry; / listen to my prayer! / From the earth's end I call to you / as my heart grows faint. / *You will set me high upon a rock; you will give me rest, / for you are my refuge, / a tower of strength against the enemy. / Oh, that I might lodge in your tent forever, / take refuge in the shelter of your wings!* / You indeed, O God, have accepted my vows; / you granted me the heritage of those who fear your name. / Add to the days of the king's life; / let his years be many generations; / Let him sit enthroned before God forever; / bid kindness and faithfulness preserve him. / So will I sing the praises of your name forever, / fulfilling my vows day by day. (Ps 61)

**Lifelong Refuge.** *O Lord, you have been our refuge / through all generations. / Before the mountains were begotten / and the earth and the world were brought forth, / from everlasting to everlasting you are God.* / You turn man back to dust, / saying, "Return, O children of men." / For a thousand years in your sight / are as yesterday, now that it is past, / or as a watch of the night. / You make an end of them in their sleep; / the next morning they are like the changing grass, / Which at dawn springs up anew, / but by evening wilts and fades. / Truly we are consumed by your anger, / and by your wrath we are put to rout. / You have kept our iniquities before you, / our hidden sins in the light of your scrutiny. / All our days have passed away in your indignation; / we have spent our years like a sigh. / Seventy is the sum of our years, / or eighty, if we are strong, / And most of them are fruitless toil, / for they pass quickly and we drift away. / Who knows the fury of your anger / or your indignation toward those who should fear you? / Teach us to number our days aright, / that we may gain wisdom of heart. / Return, O Lord! How long? / Have pity on your servants! / *Fill us at daybreak with your kindness, / that we may shout for joy and gladness all our days. / Make us glad, for the days when you afflicted us, / for the years when we saw evil.* / Let your work be seen by your servants / and your glory by their children; / And may the gracious care of the Lord our God be ours; / prosper the work of our hands for us! / [Prosper the work of our hands!] (Ps 90)

**Refuge in the Lord.** Give thanks to the Lord, for he is good, / for his mercy endures forever. / Let the house of Israel say, / "His mercy endures forever." / Let the house of Aaron say, / "His mercy endures forever." / Let those who fear the Lord say, / "His mercy endures forever." / *In my straits I called upon the Lord; / the Lord answered me and set me free.* / The Lord is with me; I fear not; / what can man do against me? / The Lord is with me to help me, / and I shall look down upon my foes. / *It is better to take refuge in the Lord / than to trust in man.* / It is better to take refuge in the Lord / than to trust in princes. / All the nations encompassed me; / in the name of the Lord I crushed them. / They encompassed me on every side; / in the name of the Lord I crushed them. / They encompassed me like bees, / they flared up like fire among thorns; / in the name of the Lord I crushed them. / *I was hard pressed and was falling, / but the Lord helped me. / My* *strength and my courage is the Lord, / and he has been my savior.* / The joyful shout of victory / in the tents of the just: / "The right hand of the Lord has struck with power: / the right hand of the Lord is exalted; / the right hand of the Lord has struck with power." / I shall not die, but live, / and declare the works of the Lord. / Though the Lord has indeed chastised me, / yet he has not delivered me to death. / Open to me the gates of justice; / I will enter them and give thanks to the Lord. / This gate is the Lord's; / the just shall enter it. / I will give thanks to you, for you have answered me / and have been my savior. / The stone which the builders rejected / has become the cornerstone. / By the Lord has this been done; / it is wonderful in our eyes. / This is the day the Lord has made; / let us be glad and rejoice in it. / O Lord, grant salvation! / O Lord, grant prosperity! / Blessed is he who comes in the name of the Lord; / we bless you from the house of the Lord. / The Lord is God, and he has given us light. / Join in procession with leafy boughs / up to the horns of the altar. / You are my God, and I give thanks to you; / O my God, I extol you. / Give thanks to the Lord, for he is good; / for his kindness endures forever. (Ps 118)

**Rock of Refuge.** Blessed be the Lord, my rock, / who trains my hands for battle, my fingers for war; / *My refuge and my fortress, / my stronghold, my deliverer, / My shield, in whom I trust, / who subdues peoples under me.* / Lord, what is man, that you notice him; / the son of man, that you take thought of him? / Man is like a breath; / his days, like a passing shadow. / Incline your heavens, O Lord, and come down; / touch the mountains, and they shall smoke; / Flash forth lightning, and put them to flight, / shoot your arrows, and rout them; / Reach out your hand from on high—/ Deliver me and rescue me from many waters, / from the hands of aliens, / Whose mouths swear false promises / while their right hands are raised in perjury. / O God, I will sing a new song to you; / with a ten-stringed lyre I will chant your praise, / You who give victory to kings, / and deliver David, your servant. / From the evil sword deliver me; / and rescue me from the hands of aliens,/ Whose mouths swear false promises / while their right hands are raised in perjury. / May our sons be like plants / well-nurtured in their youth, / Our daughters like wrought columns / such as stand at the corners of the temple. / May our garners be full, / affording every kind of store; / May our sheep be in the thousands, / and increase to myriads in our meadows; / may our oxen be well laden. / May there be no breach in the walls, no exile, / no outcry in our streets. / Happy the people for whom things are thus; / happy the people whose God is the Lord. (Ps 144)

## 19. To Plead for Protection

How eloquent the inspired writers of Scripture become when they try to tell us of God's protection! God is our shield, our rock, our refuge, our fortress. He swoops us up on eagles' wings; / he hides us in his quiver. The Lord himself says, "Fear not, I am with you; / be not dismayed; I am your God. / I will strengthen you, and help you, / and uphold you with my right hand of justice" (Is 41:10).

**No Other.** "O Lord God, you have begun to show to your servant your greatness and might. For what god in heaven or on earth can perform deeds as mighty as yours?" (Dt 3:24)

**God of Grandeur.** "Riches and honor are from you, / and you have dominion over all. / In your hand are power and might; / it is yours to give grandeur and strength to all. / Therefore, our God, we give you thanks / and we praise the majesty of your name." (1 Chr 29:12-13)

**God of Power and Might.** "Lord, God of our fathers, are you not the God in heaven, and do you not rule over all the kingdoms of the nations? In your hand is power and might, and no one can withstand you." (2 Chr 20:6)

**God of the Lowly.** "O God, my God, hear me also. . . . Your strength is not in numbers, nor does your power depend upon stalwart men; but you are the God of the lowly, the helper of the oppressed, the supporter of the weak, the protector of the forsaken, the savior of those without hope." (Jdt 9:5a, 11)

**Save Us.** "Lord, save us! We are lost!" (Mt 8:25b)

**Signs and Wonders.** "But now, O Lord, look at the threats they are leveling against us. Grant to your servants, even as they speak your words, complete assurance by stretching forth your hand in cures and signs and wonders to be worked in the name of Jesus, your holy Servant." (Acts 4:29-30)

**Solemn Promise.** *Help, O Lord! for no one now is dutiful; / faithfulness has vanished from among men.* / Everyone speaks falsehood to his neighbor; / with smooth lips they speak, and double heart. / May the Lord destroy all smooth lips / every boastful tongue, / Those who say, "We are heroes with our tongues; / our lips are our own; who is lord over us?" / "Because they rob the afflicted, and the needy sigh, / now will I arise," says the Lord; / "I will grant safety to him who longs for it." / *The promises of the Lord are sure, / like tried silver, freed from dross, sevenfold refined. / You, O Lord, will keep us / and preserve us always from this generation,* / While about us the wicked strut / and in high place are the basest of men. (Ps 12)

**Restore Your Vineyard.** O shepherd of Israel, hearken, / O guide of the flock of Joseph! / From your throne upon the cherubim, shine forth / before Ephraim, Benjamin and Manasseh. / Rouse your power, / and come to save us. / *O Lord of hosts, restore us; / if your face shine upon us, then we shall be safe.* / O Lord of hosts, how long will you burn with anger / while your people pray? / You have fed them with the bread of tears / and given them tears to drink in ample measure. / You have left us to be fought over by our neighbors, / and our enemies mock us. / O Lord of hosts, restore us; / if your face shine upon us, then we shall be safe. / A vine from Egypt you transplanted; / you drove away the nations and planted it. / You cleared the ground for it, / and it took root and filled the land. / The mountains were hidden in its shadow; / by its branches, the cedars of God. / It put forth its foliage to the Sea, / its shoots as far as the River.

/ Why have you broken down its walls, / so that every passer-by plucks its fruit, / The boar from the forest lays it waste, / and the beasts of the field feed upon it? / Once again, O Lord of hosts, / look down from heaven, and see; / Take care of this vine, / and protect what your right hand has planted / [the son of man whom you yourself made strong]. / Let those who would burn it with fire or cut it down / perish before you at your rebuke. / May your help be with the man of your right hand, / with the son of man whom you yourself made strong. / Then we will no more withdraw from you; / give us new life, and we will call upon your name. / O Lord of hosts, restore us; / if your face shine upon us, / then we shall be safe. (Ps 80)

**Secure and Protected.** You who dwell in the shelter of the Most High, / who abide in the shadow of the Almighty, / Say to the Lord, "My refuge and my fortress, / my God, in whom I trust." / For he will rescue you from the snare of the fowler, / from the destroying pestilence. / With his pinions he will cover you, / and under his wings you shall take refuge; / his faithfulness is a buckler and a shield. / You shall not fear the terror of the night/ nor the arrow that flies by day; / Not the pestilence that roams in darkness / nor the devastating plague at noon. / Though a thousand fall at your side, / ten thousand at your right side, / near you it shall not come. / Rather with your eyes shall you behold / and see the requital of the wicked. / *Because you have the Lord for your refuge; / you have made the Most High your stronghold. / No evil shall befall you, / nor shall affliction come near your tent, / For to his angels he has given command about you, /*

*that they guard you in all your ways.* / Upon their hands they shall bear you up, / lest you dash your foot against a stone. / You shall tread upon the asp and the viper, / you shall trample down the lion and the dragon. / Because he clings to me, I will deliver him; / I will set him on high because he acknowledges my name. / He shall call upon me, and I will answer him; / I will be with him in distress; / I will deliver him and glorify him; / with length of days I will gratify him / and will show him my salvation. (Ps 91)

**Faithful Protector.** They who trust in the Lord are like Mount Zion, / which is immovable; which forever stands. / Mountains are round about Jerusalem; / so the Lord is round about his people, / both now and forever. / For the scepter of the wicked shall not remain / upon the territory of the just, / Lest the just put forth / to wickedness their hands. / *Do good, O Lord, to the good / and to the upright of heart.* / But such as turn aside to crooked ways / may the Lord lead away with the evildoers! / Peace be upon Israel! (Ps 125)

## 20. *To Implore His Help in Distress*

Jesus warned us that apart from him we can do nothing, which is just another way of saying that with him we can do all things. He also promised that whatever we would ask in his name he would grant. He is pleased when we acknowledge our need of him. How comforting are his words, "Do not let your hearts be troubled. / Have faith in God / and faith in me" (Jn 14:1).

**A Mother's Plea.** "O Lord of hosts, if you look with pity on the misery of your handmaid, if you remember me and do not forget me, if you give your handmaid a male child, I will give him to the Lord for as long as he lives; neither wine nor liquor shall he drink, and no razor shall ever touch his head." (1 Sm 1:11)

**All-Powerful Lord.** "O Lord God, almighty King, all things are in your power, and there is no one to oppose you in your will.... You made heaven and earth and every wonderful thing under the heavens. You are Lord of all, and there is no one who can resist you, Lord.... Hear my prayer; have pity on your inheritance and turn our sorrow into joy: thus we shall live to sing praise to your name, O Lord. Do not silence those who praise you." (Est C:2-4, 10)

**Lest I Succumb.** Lord, Father and Master of my life, / permit me not to fall by them! / Who will apply the lash to my thoughts, / to my mind the rod of discipline, / That my failings may not be spared, / nor the sins of my heart overlooked; / Lest my failings increase, / and my sins be multiplied; / Lest I succumb to my foes, / and my enemy rejoice over me? / Lord, Father and God of my life, / abandon me not into their control! / A brazen look allow me not; / ward off passion from my heart, / Let not the lustful cravings of the flesh master me, / surrender me not to shameless desires. (Sir 23:1-6)

**No One to Console Me.** "Look, O Lord, upon my distress: / all within me is in ferment, / My heart recoils within me / from my monstrous rebellion. / In the streets the sword bereaves, / at home death stalks.

"Give heed to my groaning; / there is no one to console me." (Lam 1:20-21a)

**Be Not Deaf.** I called upon your name, O Lord, / from the bottom of the pit; / You heard me call, "Let not your ear / be deaf to my cry for help!" / You came to my aid when I called to you; / you said, "Have no fear!" / You defended me in mortal danger, / you redeemed my life. (Lam 3:55-58)

**Fervent Prayer.** "Blessed are you, and praiseworthy, / O Lord, the God of our fathers, / and glorious forever is your name. / For you are just in all you have done; / all your deeds are faultless, all your ways right, / and all your judgments proper. . . .

"For we have sinned and transgressed / by departing from you, / and we have done every kind of evil. / Your commandments we have not heeded or observed, / nor have we done as you ordered us for our good. / Therefore all you have brought upon us, / all you have done to us, / you have done by a proper judgment. . . .

"And now we follow you with our whole heart, / we fear you and we pray to you. / Do not let us be put to shame, / but deal with us in your kindness and great mercy. / Deliver us by your wonders, / and bring glory to your name, O Lord." (Dn 3:26-27, 29-31, 41-43)

**Harassment by the Wicked.** *Why, O Lord, do you stand aloof? / Why hide in times of distress? / Proudly the wicked harass the afflicted, / who are caught in the devices the wicked have contrived. / For the wicked man glories in his greed, / and the covetous blasphemes, sets the Lord* at nought. / The wicked man boasts, "He will not avenge it"; / "There is no God," sums up his thoughts. / His ways are secure at all times; / your judgments are far from his mind; / all his foes he scorns. / He says in his heart, "I shall not be disturbed; / from age to age I shall be without misfortune." / His mouth is full of cursing, guile and deceit; / under his tongue are mischief and iniquity. / He lurks in ambush near the villages; / in hiding he murders the innocent; / his eyes spy upon the unfortunate. / He waits in secret like a lion in his lair; / he lies in wait to catch the afflicted; / he catches the afflicted and drags them off in his net. / He stoops and lies prone / till by his violence fall the unfortunate. / He says in his heart, "God has forgotten; / he hides his face, he never sees." / *Rise, O Lord! O God, lift up your hand! / Forget not the afflicted!* / Why should the wicked man despise God, / saying in his heart, "He will not avenge it"? / You do see, for you behold misery and sorrow, / taking them in your hands. / On you the unfortunate man depends; / of the fatherless you are the helper. / Break the strength of the wicked and of the evildoer; / punish their wickedness; let them not survive. / The Lord is king forever and ever; / the nations have perished out of his land. / The desire of the afflicted you hear, O Lord; / strengthening their hearts, you pay heed / To the defense of the fatherless and the oppressed, / that man, who is of earth, may terrify no more. (Ps 10)

**Lamenting Corruption.** The fool says in his heart, / "There is no God." / Such are corrupt; they do abominable deeds; / there is not one who does good. / *The Lord looks down from heaven upon the children of men, / to see if there be one who is wise and seeks God.* / All alike have gone astray; they have become perverse; / there is not one who does good, not even one. / Will all these evildoers never learn, / they who eat up my people just as they eat bread? / They have not called upon the Lord; / then they shall be in great fear, / for God is with the just generation. / You would confound the plans of the afflicted, / but the Lord is his refuge. / Oh, that out of Zion would come the salvation of Israel! / When the Lord restores the well-being of his people, / then shall Jacob exult and Israel be glad. (Ps 14)

**Friend Turned Enemy.** *Hearken, O God, to my prayer; / turn not away from my pleading; / give heed to me, and answer me. / I rock with grief, and am troubled /* at the voice of the enemy and the clamor of the wicked. / For they bring down evil upon me, / and with fury they persecute me. / My heart quakes within me; / the terror of death has fallen upon me. / Fear and trembling come upon me, / and horror overwhelms me, / And I say, "Had I but wings like a dove, / I would fly away and be at rest. / Far away I would flee; / I would lodge in the wilderness. / I would hasten to find shelter / from the violent storm and the tempest." / Engulf them, O Lord; divide their counsels, / for in the city I see violence and strife; / day and night they prowl about upon its walls. / Evil and mischief are in its midst; / [treachery is in its midst;] / oppression and fraud never depart from its streets. / If an enemy had reviled me, / I could have borne it; / If he who hates me had vaunted himself against me, / I might have hidden from him. / But you, my other self, / my companion and my bosom friend! / You, whose comradeship I enjoyed; / at whose side I walked in procession in the house of God! / Let death surprise them; / let them go down alive to the nether world, / for evil is in their dwellings, in their very midst, / But I will call upon God, / and the Lord will save me. / In the evening, and at dawn, and at noon, / I will grieve and moan, / and he will hear my voice. / He will give me freedom and peace / from those who war against me, / for many there are who oppose me. / God will hear me and will humble them / from his eternal throne; / For improvement is not in them, / nor do they fear God. / Each one lays hands on his associates, / and violates his pact. / Softer than butter is his speech, / but war is in his heart; / His words are smoother than oil, / but they are drawn swords. / *Cast your care upon the Lord, / and he will support you; / never will he permit the just man to be disturbed.* / And you, O God, will bring them down / into the pit of destruction; / Men of blood and deceit shall not live out half their days. / But I trust in you, O Lord. (Ps 55)

**Just Judge.** Do you indeed like gods pronounce justice / and judge fairly, you men of rank? / Nay, you willingly commit crimes; / on earth you look to the fruits of extortion. / From the womb the wicked are perverted; / astray from birth have the liars gone. / Theirs is poison like a serpent's, / like that of a stubborn snake that stops its ears, / That it may not hear the voice of enchanters / casting cunning spells. / O God, smash their teeth in their mouths; / the jaw-teeth of the lions, break, O Lord! / Let them vanish like water flowing off; / when they draw the bow, let their arrows be headless shafts. / Let them dissolve like a melting snail, / like an untimely birth that never sees the sun. / Unexpectedly, like a thornbush, / or like thistles, let the whirlwind carry them away. / The just man shall be glad when he sees vengeance; / he shall bathe his feet in the blood of the wicked. / *And men shall say, "Truly there is a reward for the just; / truly there is a God who is judge on earth!"* (Ps 58)

**Proof of Your Favor.** *Incline your ear, O Lord; answer me, / for I am afflicted and poor. / Keep my life, for I am devoted to you; / save your servant who trusts in you. / You are my God; have pity on me, O Lord, / for to you I call all the day. / Gladden the soul of your servant, / for to you, O Lord, I lift up my soul; / For you, O Lord, are good and forgiving, / abounding in kindness to all who call upon you.* / Hearken, O Lord, to my prayer / and attend to the sound of my pleading. / In the day of my distress I call upon you, / for you will answer me. / There is none like you among the gods, O Lord, / and there are no works like yours. / All the nations you have made shall come / and worship you, O Lord, / and glorify your name. / For you are great, and you do wondrous deeds; / you alone are God. / Teach me, O Lord, your way / that I may walk in your truth; / direct my heart that it may fear your name. / I will give thanks to you, O Lord my God, / with all my heart, / and I will glorify your name forever. / Great has been your kindness toward me; / you have rescued me from the depths of the nether world. / O God, the haughty have risen up against me, / and the company of fierce men seeks my life, / nor do they set you before their eyes. / But you, O Lord, are a God merciful and gracious, / slow to anger, abounding in kindness and fidelity. / Turn toward me, and have pity on me; / give your strength to your servant, / and save the son of your handmaid. /

Grant me a proof of your favor, / that my enemies may see, to their confusion, / that you, O Lord, have helped and comforted me. (Ps 86)

**Cry in Distress.** *In my distress I called to the Lord, / and he answered me. / O Lord, deliver me from lying lip, / from treacherous tongue.* / What will he inflict on you, with more besides, / O treacherous tongue? / Sharp arrows of a warrior / with fiery coals of brushwood. / Woe is me that I sojourn in Meshech, / that I dwell amid the tents of Kedar! / All too long have I dwelt / with those who hate peace. / When I speak of peace, / they are ready for war. (Ps 120)

**Imprisoned.** *With a loud voice I cry out to the Lord; / with a loud voice I beseech the Lord. / My complaint I pour out before him; / before him I lay bare my distress.* / When my spirit is faint within me, / you know my path. / In the way along which I walk / they have hid a trap for me. / I look to the right to see, / but there is no one who pays me heed. / I have lost all means of escape; / there is no one who cares for my life. / I cry out to you, O Lord; / I say, "You are my refuge, / my portion in the land of the living." / *Attend to my cry, / for I am brought low indeed. / Rescue me from my persecutors, / for they are too strong for me.* / Lead me forth from prison, / that I may give thanks to your name. / The just shall gather around me / when you have been good to me. (Ps 142)

# 21. *For Comfort in Persecution*

It is good to know that we are never asked to suffer anything that Jesus himself has not suffered and thereby added a sanctifying value to it. In the Beatitudes Jesus assures us of this: "Blest are you when they insult and persecute you and utter every kind of slander against you because of me. Be glad and rejoice, for your reward is great in heaven" (Mt 5:11-12a).

**Arise, Lord.** "Arise, O Lord, that your enemies may be scattered, / and those who hate you may flee before you." . . . "Return, O Lord, you who ride upon the clouds." (Nm 10:35-36)

**As the Sun.** "May all your enemies perish thus, O Lord! / but your friends be as the sun rising in its might!" (Jgs 5:31)

**Look Favorably upon Me.** "Blessed are you, O Lord, merciful God! / Forever blessed and honored is your holy name; / may all your works forever bless you. / And now, O Lord, to you I turn my face / and raise my eyes. . . .

"I am my father's only daughter, / and he has no other child to make his heir. . . . look favorably upon me and have pity on me." (Tb 3:11b-12, 15)

**Strong and Just God.** "Lord, Lord God, creator of all things, awesome and strong, just and merciful, the only king and benefactor, who alone are gracious, just, almighty, and eternal, Israel's savior from all evil, who chose our forefathers and sanctified them: accept this sacrifice on behalf of all your people Israel and guard and sanctify your heritage. Gather together our scattered people, free those who are the slaves of the Gentiles, look kindly on those who are despised and detested, and let the Gentiles know that you are our God." (2 Mc 1:24-27)

**Heal Me, Lord.** Heal me, Lord, that I may be healed; / save me, that I may be saved, / for it is you whom I praise. / See how they say to me, / "Where is the word of the Lord? / Let it come to pass!" / Yet I did not press you to send calamity; / the day without remedy I have not desired. / You know what passed my lips; / it is present before you. / Do not be my ruin, / you, my refuge in the day of misfortune. (Jer 17:14-17)

**How Long, O Lord?** How long, O Lord? I cry for help / but you do not listen! / I cry out to you, "Violence!" / but you do not intervene. / Why do you let me see ruin; / why must I look at misery? / Destruction and violence are before me; / there is strife, and clamorous discord. (Hb 1:2-3)

**God Saves.** How long, O Lord? Will you utterly forget me? / How long will you hide your face from me? / How long shall I harbor sorrow in my soul, / grief in my heart day after day? / How long will my enemy triumph over me? / Look, answer me, O Lord, my God! / Give light to my eyes that I may not sleep in death / lest my enemy say, "I have overcome him"; / Lest my foes rejoice at my downfall / though I trusted in your kindness. / Let my heart rejoice in your salvation; / *let me sing of the Lord, "He has been good to me."* (Ps 13)

**Unjust Enemies.** Fight, O Lord, against those who fight me; / war against those who make war upon me. / Take up the shield and buckler, / and rise up in my defense. / Brandish the lance, and block the way / in the face of my pursuers; / Say to my soul, / "I am your salvation." / Let those be put to shame and disgraced who seek my life; /

Let those be turned back and confounded / who plot evil against me. / Let them be like chaff before the wind, / with the angel of the Lord driving them on. / Let their way be dark and slippery, / with the angel of the Lord pursuing them. / For without cause they set their snare for me, / without cause they dug a pit against my life. / Let ruin come upon them unawares, / and let the snare they have set catch them; / into the pit they have dug let them fall. / *But I will rejoice in the Lord, / I will be joyful because of his salvation. / All my being shall say, / "O Lord, who is like you, / The rescuer of the afflicted man from those too strong for him, / of the afflicted and the needy from their despoilers?"* / Unjust witnesses have risen up; / things I knew not of, they lay to my charge. / They have repaid me evil for good, / bringing bereavement to my soul. / But I, when they were ill, put on sackcloth; / I afflicted myself with fasting / and poured forth prayers within my bosom. / As though it were a friend of mine, or a brother, I went about; / like one bewailing a mother, I was bowed down in mourning. / Yet when I stumbled they were glad and gathered together; / they gathered together striking me unawares. / They tore at me without ceasing; / they put me to the test; they mocked me, / gnashing their teeth at me. / O Lord, how long will you look on? / Save me from the roaring beasts; from the lions, my only life. / I will give you thanks in the vast assembly, / in the mighty throng I will praise you. / Let not my unprovoked enemies rejoice over me; / let not my undeserved foes wink knowingly. / For civil words they speak not, / but against the peaceful in the land / they fashion treacherous speech. / And they open wide their mouths against me, / saying, "Aha, aha! we saw him with our own eyes!" / You, O Lord, have seen; be not silent; / Lord, be not far from me! / *Awake, and be vigilant in my defense; / in my cause, my God and my Lord.* / Do me justice, because you are just, O Lord; / my God, let them not rejoice over me. / Let them not say in their hearts, "Aha! This is what we wanted!" / Let them not say, "We have swallowed him up!" / Let all be put to shame and confounded / who are glad at my misfortune. / Let those be clothed with shame and disgrace / who glory over me. / But let those shout for joy and be glad / who favor my just cause; / And may they ever say, "The Lord be glorified; / he wills the prosperity of his servant!" / Then my tongue shall recount your justice, / your praise, all the day. (Ps 35)

**Our Stronghold.** Rescue me from my enemies, O my God; / from my adversaries defend me. / Rescue me from evildoers; / from bloodthirsty men save me. / For behold, they lie in wait for my life; / mighty men come together against me. / Not for any offense or sin of mine, O Lord; / for no guilt of mine they hurry to take up arms. / Rouse yourself to see it, and aid me, / for you are the Lord of hosts, the God of Israel. / Arise; punish all the nations; / have no pity on any worthless traitors. / Each evening they return, they snarl like dogs / and prowl about the city. / Though they bay with their mouths, / and blasphemies are on their lips— / "Who is there to listen?"— / You, O Lord, laugh at them; / you deride all the nations. / *O my strength! for you I watch; / for you, O God, are my stronghold, / my gracious God! / May God come to my aid; / may he show me the fall of my foes.* / O God, slay them, lest they beguile my people; / shake them by your power, and bring them down, / O Lord our shield! / By the sin of their mouths and the word of their lips / let them be caught in their arrogance, / for the lies they have told under oath. / Consume them in wrath; consume, till they are no more; / that men may know that God is the ruler of Jacob, / yes, to the ends of the earth. / Each evening they return, they snarl like dogs / and prowl about the city; / They wander about as scavengers; / if they are not filled, they howl. / *But I will sing of your strength / and revel at dawn in your kindness; / You have been my stronghold, / my refuge in the day of distress. / O my strength! your praise will I sing; / for you, O God, are my stronghold, / my gracious God!* (Ps 59)

**Cry for Relief.** O God, the nations have come into your inheritance; / they have defiled your holy temple, / they have laid Jerusalem in ruins. / They have given the corpses of your servants / as food to the birds of heaven, / the flesh of your faithful ones to the beasts of the earth. / They have poured out their blood like water round about Jerusalem, / and there is no one to bury them. / We have become the reproach of our neighbors, / the scorn and derision of those around us. / O Lord, how long? Will you be angry forever? / Will your jealousy burn like fire? / Pour out your wrath upon the nations that acknowledge you not, / upon the kingdoms that call not upon your name; / For they have devoured Jacob / and laid waste his dwelling. / *Remember not against us the iniquities of the past; / may your compassion quickly come to us; / for we are brought very low. / Help us, O God our savior, / because of the glory of your name; / Deliver us and pardon our sins / for your name's sake.* / Why should the nations say, / "Where is their God?" / Let it be known among the nations in our sight / that you avenge the shedding of your servants' blood. / Let the prisoners' sighing come before you; / with your great power free those doomed to death. / And repay our neighbors sevenfold into their bosoms / the disgrace they have inflicted on you, O Lord. / Then we, your people and the sheep of your pasture, / will give thanks to you forever; / through all generations we will declare your praise. (Ps 79)

**Recompense.** O God, whom I praise, be not silent, / for they have opened wicked and treacherous mouths against me. / They have spoken to me with lying tongues, / and with words of hatred they have encompassed me / and attacked me without cause. / In return for my love they slandered me, / but I prayed. / They repaid me evil for good / and hatred for my love. / Raise up a wicked man against him, / and let the accuser stand at his right hand. / When he is judged, let him go forth condemned, / and may his plea be in vain. / May his days be few; / may another take his office. / May his children be fatherless, / and his wife a widow. / May his children be roaming vagrants and beggars; / may they be cast out of the ruins of their homes. / May the usurer ensnare all his belongings, / and strangers plunder the fruit of his labors. / May there be no one to do him a kindness, / nor anyone to pity his orphans. / May his posterity meet with destruction; / in the next generation may their name be blotted out. / May the guilt of his father be remembered by the Lord; / let not his mother's sin be blotted out; / May they be continually before the Lord, / till he banish the memory of these parents from the earth, / Because he remembered not to show kindness, / but persecuted the wretched and poor / and the brokenhearted, to do them to death. / He loved cursing; may it come upon him; / he took no delight in blessing; may it be far from him. / And may he be clothed with cursing as with a robe; / may it penetrate into his entrails like water, and like oil into his bones; / May it be for him like a garment which covers him, / like a girdle which is always about him. / May this be the recompense from the Lord upon my accusers / and upon those who speak evil against me. / *But do you, O God, my Lord, deal kindly with me for your name's sake; / in your generous kindness rescue me;* / For I am wretched and poor, / and my heart is pierced within me. / Like a lengthening shadow I pass away; / I am swept away like the locust. / My knees totter from my fasting, / and my flesh is wasted of its substance. / And I am become a mockery to them; / when they see me, they shake their heads. / Help me, O Lord, my God; / save me, in your kindness, / And let them know that this is your hand, / that you, O Lord, have done this. / Let them curse, but do you bless; / may my adversaries be put to shame, / but let your servant rejoice. / Let my accusers be clothed with disgrace / and let them wear their shame like a mantle. / *I will speak my thanks earnestly to the Lord, / and in the midst of the throng I will praise him, / For he stood at the right hand of the poor man, / to save him from those who would condemn him.* (Ps 109)

## 22. To Overcome Fear

Some kind of fear is latent in all of us, because we all have some feelings of insecurity. This is why we are advised so frequently in the Scriptures, "Do not be afraid," "Fear is useless," "Fear not!" St. John gives us the panacea, "Love has no room for fear; rather, perfect love casts out all fear" (1 Jn 4:18).

**Hold Not Back.** Look down from heaven and regard us / from your holy and glorious palace! / Where is your zealous care and your might, / your surge of pity and your mercy? / O Lord, hold not back, / for you are our father. (Is 63:15-16a)

**He Is Trustworthy.** May the God of peace make you perfect in holiness. May he preserve you whole and entire, spirit, soul, and body, irreproachable at the coming of our Lord Jesus Christ. He who calls us is trustworthy, therefore he will do it. (1 Thes 5:23-24)

**Rule in Love.** May the Lord rule your hearts in the love of God and the constancy of Christ. (2 Thes 3:5)

**Loving Care.** Sin speaks to the wicked man in his heart; / there is no dread of God before his eyes, / For he beguiles himself with the thought / that his guilt will not be found out or hated. / The words of his mouth are empty and false; / he has ceased to understand how to do good. / He plans wickedness in his bed; / he sets out on a way that is not good, with no repugnance for evil. / O Lord, your kindness reaches to heaven; / your faithfulness, to the clouds. / Your justice is like the mountains of God; / your judgments, like the mighty deep; / man and beast you save, O Lord. / *How precious is your kindness, O God! / The children of men take refuge in the shadow of your wings. / They have their fill of the prime gifts of your house; / from your delightful stream you give them to drink. / For with you is the*

*fountain of life, / and in your light we see light.* / Keep up
your kindness toward your friends, / your just defense of
the upright of heart. / Let not the foot of the proud
overtake me / nor the hand of the wicked disquiet me. /
See how the evildoers have fallen; / they are thrust down
and cannot rise. (Ps 36)

**Fear Not the Wicked.** Hear this, all you peoples; /
hearken, all who dwell in the world, / Of lowly birth or
high degree, / rich and poor alike. / My mouth shall
speak wisdom; / prudence shall be the utterance of my
heart. / My ear is intent upon a proverb; / I will set forth
my riddle to the music of the harp. / Why should I fear in
evil days / when my wicked ensnarers ring me round? /
They trust in their wealth; / the abundance of their riches
is their boast. / Yet in no way can a man redeem himself, /
or pay his own ransom to God; / Too high is the price to
redeem one's life; he would never have enough / to
remain alive always and not see destruction. / For he can
see that wise men die, / and likewise the senseless and the
stupid pass away, / leaving to others their wealth. /
Tombs are their homes forever, / their dwellings
through all generations, / though they have called lands
by their names. / Thus man, for all his splendor, does not
abide; / he resembles the beasts that perish. / This is the
way of those whose trust is folly, / the end of those
contented with their lot: / Like sheep they are herded
into the nether world; / death is their shepherd, and the
upright rule over them. / Quickly their form is consumed; / the nether world is their palace. / *But God will
redeem me / from the power of the nether world by receiving
me.* / Fear not when a man grows rich, / when the wealth
of his house becomes great, / For when he dies, he shall

take none of it; / his wealth shall not follow him down. / Thus in his lifetime he counted himself blessed. / "They will praise you for doing well for yourself," / He shall join the circle of his forebears / who shall never more see light. / Man, for all his splendor, if he have not prudence, / resembles the beasts that perish. (Ps 49)

**A Fool's Taunt.** The fool says in his heart, / "There is no God." / Such are corrupt; they do abominable deeds; / there is not one who does good. / *God looks down from heaven upon the children of men / to see if there be one who is wise and seeks God.* / All alike have gone astray; they have become perverse; / there is not one who does good, not even one. / Will all these evildoers never learn, / they who eat up my people just as they eat bread, / who call not upon God? / There they were in great fear, / where no fear was, / for God has scattered the bones of your besiegers; / they are put to shame, because God has rejected them. / Oh, that out of Zion would come the salvation of Israel! / When God restores the well-being of his people, / then shall Jacob exult and Israel be glad. (Ps 53)

**Plea for Help.** O God, you have rejected us and broken our defenses; / you have been angry; rally us! / You have rocked the country and split it open; / repair the cracks in it, for it is tottering. / You have made your people feel hardships; / you have given us stupefying wine. / You have raised for those who fear you a banner / to which they may flee out of bowshot / That your loved ones may escape; / help us by your right hand, and answer us! / God promised in his sanctuary: / "Exultantly I will apportion Shechem, / and measure off the valley of Succoth. / Mine is Gilead, and mine Manasseh; / Ephraim is the helmet for my head; Judah, my scepter; / Moab shall serve as my washbowl; / upon Edom I will set my shoe; / I will triumph over Philistia." / Who will bring me into the fortified city? / Who will lead me into Edom? / Have not you, O God, rejected us, / so that you go not forth, O God, with our armies? / *Give us aid against the foe, / for worthless is the help of men. / Under God we shall do valiantly; / it is he who will tread down our foes.* (Ps 60)

**He Raises the Lowly.** Praise, you servants of the Lord, / praise the name of the Lord. / Blessed be the name of the Lord / both now and forever. / From the rising to the setting of the sun / is the name of the Lord to be praised. / *High above all nations is the Lord; / above the heavens is his glory. / Who is like the Lord, our God, who is enthroned on high / and looks upon the heavens and the earth below?* / He raises up the lowly from the dust; / from the dunghill he lifts up the poor / To seat them with princes, / with the princes of his own people. / He establishes in her home the barren wife / as the joyful mother of children. (Ps 113)

## 23. To Accept Life's Infirmities

"He comforts us in all our afflictions and thus enables us to comfort those who are in trouble, with the same consolation we have received from him. As we have shared much in the suffering of Christ, so through Christ do we share abundantly in his consolation. If we are afflicted it is for your encouragement and salvation, and when we are consoled it is for your consolation, so that you may endure patiently the same sufferings we endure" (2 Cor 1:4-6).

**No Terror.** These things only do not use against me, / then from your presence I need not hide: / Withdraw your hand far from me, / and let not the terror of you frighten me. / Then call me, and I will respond; / or let me speak first, and answer me. / What are my faults and my sins? / My misdeeds and my sins make known to me! / Why do you hide your face / and consider me your enemy? / Will you harass a wind-driven leaf, / or pursue a withered straw? (Jb 13:20-25)

**Like a Shepherd's Tent.** Once I said, / "In the noontime of life I must depart! / To the gates of the nether world I shall be consigned / for the rest of my years." / I said, "I shall see the Lord no more / in the land of the living. / No longer shall I behold my fellow men / among those who dwell in the world." / My dwelling, like a shepherd's tent, / is struck down and borne away from me; / You have folded up my life, like a weaver / who severs the last thread. / Day and night you give me over to torment; / I cry out until the dawn. / Like a lion he breaks all my bones; / [day and night you give me over to torment]. / Like a swallow I utter shrill cries; / I moan like a dove. / My eyes grow weak, gazing heavenward: / O Lord, I am in straits; be my surety! (Is 38:10-14)

**Have Pity.** As Jesus moved on from there, two blind men came after him crying out, "Son of David, have pity on us!" (Mt 9:27)

**God of Consolation.** Praised be God, the Father of our Lord Jesus Christ, the Father of mercies, and the God of all consolation! He comforts us in all our afflictions and thus enables us to comfort those who are in trouble, with the same consolation we have received from him. (2 Cor 1:3-4)

**Brevity of Life.** I said, "I will watch my ways, / so as not to sin with my tongue; / I will set a curb on my mouth." / While the wicked man was before me / I kept dumb and silent; / I refrained from rash speech. / But my grief was stirred up; / hot grew my heart within me; / in my thoughts, a fire blazed forth. / I spoke out with my tongue: / Let me know, O Lord, my end / and what is the number of my days, / that I may learn how frail I am. / A short span you have made my days, / and my life is as nought before you; / only a breath is any human existence. / A phantom only, man goes his ways; / like vapor only are his restless pursuits; / he heaps up stores, and knows not who will use them. / *And now, for what do I wait, O Lord? / In you is my hope. / From all my sins deliver me; / a fool's taunt let me not suffer.* / I was speechless and opened not my mouth, / because it was your doing; / Take away your scourge from me; / at the blow of your hand I wasted away. / With rebukes for guilt you chasten man; / you dissolve like a cobweb all that is dear to him; / only a breath is any man. / *Hear my prayer, O Lord; / to my cry give ear; / to my weeping be not deaf! / For I am but a wayfarer before you, / a pilgrim like all my fathers.* / Turn your gaze from me, that I may find respite / ere I depart and be no more. (Ps 39)

**Trust in Old Age.** In you, O Lord, I take refuge; / let me never be put to shame. / In your justice rescue me, and deliver me; / incline your ear to me, and save me. / Be my rock of refuge, / a stronghold to give me safety, / for you are my rock and my fortress. / O my God, rescue me from the hand of the wicked, / from the grasp of the criminal and the violent. / *For you are my hope, O Lord; / my trust, O God, from my youth. / On you I depend from birth; / from my mother's womb you are my strength; / constant has been my hope in you.* / A portent am I to many, / but you are my strong refuge! / My mouth shall be filled with your praise, / with your glory day by day. / *Cast me not off in my old age; / as my strength fails, forsake me not,* / For my enemies speak against me, / and they who keep watch against my life take counsel together. / They say, "God has forsaken him; / pursue and seize him, / for there is no one to rescue him." / O God, be not far from me; / my God, make haste to help me. / Let them be put to shame and consumed who attack my life; / let them be wrapped in ignominy and disgrace who seek to harm me. / But I will always hope / and praise you ever more and more. / My mouth shall declare your justice, / day by day your salvation, / though I know not their extent. / I will treat of the mighty works of the Lord; / O God, I will tell of your singular justice. / *O God, you have taught me from my youth, / and till the present I proclaim your wondrous deeds; / And now that I am old and gray, / O God, forsake me not / Till I proclaim your strength / to every generation that is to come.* / Your power and your justice, / O God, reach to heaven. / You have done great things; / O God, who is like you? / Though you have made me feel many bitter afflictions, / you will again revive me; / from the depths of the earth you will once more raise me. / Renew your benefits toward me, / and comfort me over and over. /

So will I give you thanks with music on the lyre, / for your faithfulness, O my God! / I will sing your praises with the harp, / O Holy One of Israel! / My lips shall shout for joy / as I sing your praises; / My soul also, which you have redeemed, / and my tongue day by day shall discourse / on your justice. / How shamed and how disgraced / are those who sought to harm me! (Ps 71)

**Mortal Illness.** *O Lord, my God, by day I cry out; / at night I clamor in your presence.* / Let my prayer come before you; / incline your ear to my call for help, / For my soul is surfeited with troubles / and my life draws near to the nether world. / I am numbered with those who go down into the pit; / I am a man without strength. / My couch is among the dead, / like the slain who lie in the grave, / Whom you remember no longer / and who are cut off from your care. / You have plunged me into the bottom of the pit, / into the dark abyss. / Upon me your wrath lies heavy, / and with all your billows you overwhelm me. / You have taken my friends away from me; / you have made me an abomination to them; / I am imprisoned, and I cannot escape. / *My eyes have grown dim through affliction; / daily I call upon you, O Lord; / to you I stretch out my hands.* / Will you work wonders for the dead? / Will the shades arise to give you thanks? / Do they declare your kindness in the grave, / your faithfulness among those who have perished? / Are your wonders made known in the darkness, / or your justice in the land of oblivion? / *But I, O Lord, cry out to you; / with my morning prayer I wait upon you.* / Why, O Lord, do you reject me; / why hide from me your face? / I am afflicted and in agony from my youth; / I am dazed with the burden of your dread. / Your furies have swept over me; / your terrors have cut me off. / They encompass me like water all the day; / on all sides they close in upon me. / Companion and neighbor you have take away from me; / my only friend is darkness. (Ps 88)

# 24. For Joyous Journeying

Christians must be emissaries of the good news. Their mission is to bring joy to others by proclaiming the good news as they journey along. Being informed and formed by the good news, they recognize it as the only genuine source of joy, as Jesus himself said, "All this I tell you that my joy may be yours and your joy may be complete" (Jn 15:11).

**Come with Us.** "If I find favor with you, O Lord, do come along in our company. This is indeed a stiff-necked people; yet pardon our wickedness and sins, and receive us as your own." (Ex 34:9)

**Dependable Guide.** Now God grant I speak suitably / and value these endowments at their worth: / For he is the guide of Wisdom / and the director of the wise. / For both we and our words are in his hand, / as well as all prudence and knowledge of crafts. (Wis 7:15-16)

**Lead Us Back.** You, O Lord, are enthroned forever; / your throne stands from age to age. / Why, then, should you forget us, / abandon us so long a time? / Lead us back to you, O Lord, that we may be restored: / give us anew such days as we had of old. (Lam 5:19-21)

**Always with Us.** The grace of the Lord Jesus Christ, and the love of God, and the fellowship of the Holy Spirit be with you all! (2 Cor 13:13)

**Faithful Guardian.** *I lift up my eyes toward the mountains; / whence shall help come to me? / My help is from the Lord, / who made heaven and earth.* / May he not suffer your foot to slip; / May he slumber not who guards you: / Indeed he neither slumbers nor sleeps, / the guardian of Israel. / The Lord is your guardian; the Lord is your shade; / he is beside you at your right hand. / The sun shall not harm you by day, / nor the moon by night. / *The Lord will guard you from all evil; / he will guard your life. / The Lord will guard your coming and your going, / Both now and forever.* (Ps 121)

**On to His House.** *I rejoiced because they said to me, / "We will go up to the house of the Lord."* / And now we have set foot / within your gates, O Jerusalem— / Jerusalem, built as a city / with compact unity. / To it the tribes go up, / the tribes of the Lord, / According to the decree for Israel, / to give thanks to the name of the Lord. / In it are set up judgment seats, / seats for the house of David. / Pray for the peace of Jerusalem! / May those who love you prosper! / May peace be within your walls, / prosperity in your buildings. / Because of my relatives and friends / I will say, "Peace be within you!" / Because of the house of the Lord, our God, / I will pray for your good. (Ps 122)

**Safe at Last.** Had not the Lord been with us, / let Israel say, / had not the Lord been with us— / When men rose up against us, / then would they have swallowed us alive. / When their fury was inflamed against us, / then would the waters have overwhelmed us; / The torrent would have swept over us; / over us then would have swept / the raging waters. / *Blessed be the Lord, who did not leave us / a prey to their teeth. / We were rescued like a bird / from the fowlers' snare; / Broken was the snare, / and we were freed.* / Our help is in the name of the Lord, / who made heaven and earth. (Ps 124)

**Home.** When the Lord brought back the captives of Zion, / we were like men dreaming. / Then our mouth was filled with laughter, / and our tongue with rejoicing. / Then they said among the nations, / "The Lord has done great things for them." / The Lord has done great things for us; / we are glad indeed. / Restore our fortunes, O Lord, / like the torrents in the southern desert. / *Those that sow in tears / shall reap rejoicing. / Although they go forth weeping, / carrying the seed to be sown, / They shall come back rejoicing, / carrying their sheaves.* (Ps 126)

## 25. To Find Our Joy in the Lord

Every human being wants to be happy and joyous. Unfortunately, some seek happiness via an escape route, dissipation, drugs, pleasure, hyperactivity. None of these can satisfy the human heart. Only a deep personal relationship with the Lord can bring us genuine joy. St. Paul is direct in his encouragement, "Rejoice in the Lord always! I say it again. Rejoice! Everyone should see how unselfish you are. The Lord is near" (Phil 4:4-5).

**Wherever You Go.** "Do not ask me to abandon or forsake you! for wherever you go I will go, wherever you lodge I will lodge, your people shall be my people, and your God my God. Wherever you die I will die, and there be buried. May the Lord do so and so to me, and more besides, if aught but death separates me from you!" (Ru 1:16-17)

**Rebuilt with Joy.** Praise the Lord for his goodness, / and bless the King of the ages, / so that his tent may be rebuilt in you with joy. / May he gladden within you all who were captives; / all who were ravaged may he cherish within you / for all generations to come.

A bright light will shine to all parts of the earth; / many nations shall come to you from afar, / And the inhabitants of all the limits of the earth, / drawn to you by the name of the Lord God, / Bearing in their hands their gifts / for the King of heaven. / Every generation shall give joyful praise in you, / and shall call you the chosen one, / through all ages forever. / Accursed are all who speak a harsh word against you; / accursed are all who destroy you / and pull down your walls, / And all who overthrow your towers / and set fire to your homes; / but forever blessed are all those who build you up.

Go, then, rejoice over the children of the righteous, / who shall all be gathered together / and shall bless the Lord of the ages. / Happy are those who love you, / and happy those who rejoice in your prosperity.

Happy are all the men who shall grieve over you, / over all your chastisements. / For they shall rejoice in you / as they behold all your joy forever.

My spirit bless the Lord, the great King; / Jerusalem shall be rebuilt as his home forever. / Happy for me if a remnant of my offspring survive / to see your glory and to praise the King of heaven!

The gates of Jerusalem shall be built with sapphire and emerald, / and all your walls with precious stones. / The towers of Jerusalem shall be built with gold, / and their battlements with pure gold.

The streets of Jerusalem shall be paved / with rubies and stones of Ophir; / The gates of Jerusalem shall sing hymns of gladness, / and all her houses shall cry out, "Alleluia!"

"Blessed be God who has raised you up! / may he be blessed for all ages!" / For in you they shall praise his holy name forever. (Tb 13:10-18)

**Joy of My Soul.** I rejoice heartily in the Lord, / in my God is the joy of my soul; / For he has clothed me with a robe of salvation, / and wrapped me in a mantle of justice, / Like a bridegroom adorned with a diadem, / like a bride bedecked with her jewels. / As the earth brings forth its plants, / and a garden makes its growth spring up, / So will the Lord God make justice and praise / spring up before all the nations. (Is 61:10-11)

**I Will Return.** If you allow me, I will return, / for you are the Lord, my God. / I turn in repentance; / I have come to myself, I strike my breast; / I blush with shame, / I bear the disgrace of my youth. (Jer 31:18b-19)

**Source of Joy.** "Blessed be the name of God forever and ever, / for wisdom and power are his. / He causes the changes of the times and seasons, / makes kings and unmakes them. / He gives wisdom to the wise / and knowledge to those who understand. / He reveals deep and hidden things / and knows what is in the darkness, / for the light dwells with him. / To you, O God of my fathers, / I give thanks and praise, / because you have given me wisdom and power. (Dan 2:20-23a)

**Fullness of Joy.** Keep me, O God, for in you I take refuge; / I say to the Lord, "My Lord are you. / Apart from you I have no good." / How wonderfully has he made me cherish / the holy ones who are in his land! / They multiply their sorrows / who court other gods. / Blood libations to them I will not pour out, / nor will I take their names upon my lips. / O Lord, my allotted portion and my cup, / you it is who hold fast my lot. / For me the measuring lines have fallen on pleasant sites; / fair to me indeed is my inheritance. / I bless the Lord who counsels me; / even in the night my heart exhorts me. / I set the Lord ever before me; / with him at my right hand I shall not be disturbed. / Therefore my heart is glad and my soul rejoices, / my body, too, abides in confidence; / Because you will not abandon my soul to the nether world, / nor will you suffer your faithful one to undergo corruption. / *You will show me the path of life, / fullness of joys in your presence, / the delights at your right hand forever.* (Ps 16)

**Radiant Joy.** I will bless the Lord at all times; / his praise shall be ever in my mouth. / Let my soul glory in the Lord; / the lowly will hear me and be glad. / Glorify the Lord with me, / let us together extol his name. / I sought the Lord, and he answered me / and delivered me from all my fears. / *Look to him that you may be radiant with joy, /*

*and your faces may not blush with shame.* / When the afflicted man called out, the Lord heard, / and from all his distress he saved him. / The angel of the Lord encamps / around those who fear him, and delivers them. / *Taste and see how good the Lord is;* / *happy the man who takes refuge in him.* / Fear the Lord, you his holy ones, / for nought is lacking to those who fear him. / The great grow poor and hungry; / but those who seek the Lord want for no good thing. / Come, children, hear me; / I will teach you the fear of the Lord. / Which of you desires life, / and takes delight in prosperous days? / Keep your tongue from evil / and your lips from speaking guile; / Turn from evil, and do good; / seek peace, and follow after it. / The Lord has eyes for the just, / and ears for their cry. / The Lord confronts the evildoers, / to destroy remembrance of them from the earth. / When the just cry out, the Lord hears them, / and from all their distress he rescues them. / The Lord is close to the brokenhearted; / and those who are crushed in spirit he saves. / Many are the troubles of the just man, / but out of them all the Lord delivers him; / He watches over all his bones; / not one of them shall be broken. / Vice slays the wicked, / and the enemies of the just pay for their guilt. / But the Lord redeems the lives of his servants; / no one incurs guilt who takes refuge in him. (Ps **34**)

**Melodious Joy.** *Sing joyfully to God our strength;* / *acclaim the God of Jacob.* / Take up a melody, and sound the timbrel, / the pleasant harp and the lyre. / Blow the trumpet at the new moon, / at the full moon, on our solemn feast; / For it is a statute in Israel, / an ordinance of the God of Jacob, / Who made it a decree for Joseph

/ when he came forth from the land of Egypt. / An unfamiliar speech I hear: / "I relieved his shoulder of the burden; / his hands were freed from the basket. / In distress you called, and I rescued you; / Unseen, I answered you in thunder; / I tested you at the waters of Meribah. / Hear, my people, and I will admonish you; / O Israel, will you not hear me? / There shall be no strange god among you / nor shall you worship any alien god. / I, the Lord, am your God / who led you forth from the land of Egypt; / open wide your mouth, and I will fill it. / But my people heard not my voice, / and Israel obeyed me not; / So I gave them up to the hardness of their hearts; / they walked according to their own counsels. / If only my people would hear me, / and Israel walk in my ways, / Quickly would I humble their enemies; / against their foes I would turn my hand. / Those who hated the Lord would seek to flatter me, / but their fate would endure forever, / *While Israel I would feed with the best of wheat, / and with honey from the rock I would fill them.*" (Ps 81)

**Peace and Joy.** You have favored, O Lord, your land; / you have restored the well-being of Jacob. / You have forgiven the guilt of your people; / you have covered all their sins. / You have withdrawn all your wrath; / you have revoked your burning anger. / Restore us, O God our savior, / and abandon your displeasure against us. / Will you be ever angry with us, / prolonging your anger to all generations? / *Will you not instead give us life; / and shall not your people rejoice in you? / Show us, O Lord, your kindness, / and grant us your salvation.* / I will hear what God proclaims; / the Lord—for he proclaims peace. /

To his people, and to his faithful ones, / and to those who put in him their hope. / Near indeed is his salvation to those who fear him, / glory dwelling in our land. / Kindness and truth shall meet; / justice and peace shall kiss. / Truth shall spring out of the earth, / and justice shall look down from heaven. / The Lord himself will give his benefits; / our land shall yield its increase. / Justice shall walk before him, / and salvation, along the way of his steps. (Ps 85)

## 26. For a Happy Home

The simple home at Nazareth must have been a superbly happy household, because all the members were attuned to God's heart and will. Jesus is present not only in our home but in every member of our family. St. Paul's admonition is right: "Bear with one another; forgive whatever grievances you have against one another. Forgive as the Lord has forgiven you. Over all these virtues put on love, which binds the rest together and makes them perfect" (Col 3:13-14).

**Bless this House.** "Do, then, bless the house of your servant that it may be before you forever; for you, Lord God, have promised, and by your blessing the house of your servant shall be blessed forever." (2 Sm 7:29)

**Love Creates.** "Blessed are you, O God of our fathers; / praised be your name forever and ever. / Let the heavens and all your creation / praise you forever. / You made Adam and you gave him his wife Eve / to be his help and support; / and from these two the human race descended. / You said, 'It is not good for the man to be alone; / let us make him a partner like himself.' / Now, Lord, you know that I take this wife of mine / not because of lust, / but for a noble purpose. / Call down your mercy on me and on her, / and allow us to live together to a happy old age." (Tb 8:5b-7)

**Toward Fulfillment.** "Blessed are you, O God, with every holy and pure blessing! / Let all your chosen ones praise you; / let them bless you forever! / Blessed are you, who have made me glad; / what I feared did not happen. / Rather you have dealt with us / according to your great mercy. / Blessed are you, for you were merciful / toward two only children. / Grant them, Master, mercy and deliverance, / and bring their lives to fulfillment / with happiness and mercy." (Tb 8:15b-17)

**Live in Harmony.** May God, the source of all patience and encouragement, enable you to live in perfect harmony with one another according to the spirit of Christ Jesus, so that with one heart and voice you may glorify God, the Father of our Lord Jesus Christ. (Rom 15:5-6)

**The Lord's House.** *Unless the Lord build the house, / they labor in vain who build it. / Unless the Lord guard the city, / in vain does the guard keep vigil.* / It is vain for you to rise early, / or put off your rest, / You that eat hard-earned bread, / for he gives to his beloved in sleep. / Behold, sons are a gift from the Lord; / the fruit of the womb is a reward. / Like arrows in the hand of a warrior / are the sons of one's youth. / Happy the man whose quiver is filled with them; / they shall not be put to shame when they contend / with enemies at the gate. (Ps 127)

**Blessings of Family Life.** *Happy are you who fear the Lord, / who walk in his ways!* / For you shall eat the fruit of your handiwork; / happy shall you be, and favored. / Your wife shall be like a fruitful vine / in the recesses of your home; / Your children like olive plants / around your table. / Behold, thus is the man blessed / who fears the Lord. / The Lord bless you from Zion: / may you see the prosperity of Jerusalem / all the days of your life; / May you see your children's children. / Peace be upon Israel! (Ps 128)

**Love One Another.** *Behold, how good it is, and how pleasant, / where brethren dwell at one!* / It is as when the precious ointment upon the head / runs down over the beard, the beard of Aaron, / till it runs down upon the collar of his robe. / It is a dew like that of Hermon, / which comes down upon the mountains of Zion; / For there the Lord has pronounced his blessing, / life forever. (Ps 133)

## 27. To Intercede for Others

One of the shortest and perhaps the most difficult law that Jesus gave us is "Love your neighbor as yourself." There are countless ways of manifesting our love of neighbor. A powerful way of expressing our love is by praying for all our brothers and sisters, begging the Lord to continue to bless them abundantly. Jesus said it very clearly: "My command to you is: love your enemies, pray for your persecutors. This will prove that you are sons of your heavenly Father, for his sun rises on the bad and the good, he rains on the just and the unjust" (Mt 5:44-45).

**Your Own People.** "Now, if I have found favor with you, do let me know your ways so that, in knowing you, I may continue to find favor with you. Then, too, this nation is, after all, your own people." (Ex 33:13)

**Reject Not Our Plea.** "Forgive your people who have sinned against you. My God, may your eyes be open and your ears attentive to the prayer of this place. And now, / 'Advance, Lord God, to your resting place, / you and the ark of your majesty. / May your priests, Lord God, be clothed with salvation, / may your faithful ones rejoice in good things. / Lord God, reject not the plea of your anointed.'" (2 Chr 6:39b-42a)

**Prayer for Deliverance.** "Lord, Son of David, have pity on me! My daughter is terribly troubled by a demon." (Mt 15:22)

**All Blessings.** I pray that he will bestow on you gifts in keeping with the riches of his glory. May he strengthen you inwardly through the working of his Spirit. May Christ dwell in your hearts through faith, and may charity be the root and foundation of your life. Thus you will be able to grasp fully, with all the holy ones, the breadth and length and height and depth of Christ's love, and experience this love which surpasses all knowledge, so that you may attain to the fullness of God himself.

To him whose power now at work in us can do immeasurably more than we ask or imagine—to him be glory in the church and in Christ Jesus through all generations, world without end. Amen. (Eph 3:16-21)

**Grant Success.** The Lord answer you in time of distress; / the name of the God of Jacob defend you! / May he send you help from the sanctuary, / from Zion may he sustain you. / May he remember all your offerings / and graciously accept your holocaust. / *May he grant you what is in your heart / and fulfill your every plan. / May we shout for joy at your victory / and raise the standards in the name of our God. / The Lord grant all your requests!* / Now I know that the Lord has given victory to his anointed, / that he has answered him from his holy heaven / with the strength of his victorious right hand. / Some are strong in chariots; some, in horses; / but we are strong in the name of the Lord, our God. / Though they bow down and fall, / yet we stand erect and firm. / O Lord, grant victory to the king, / and answer us when we call upon you. (Ps 20)

**Bold Plea.** O God, our ears have heard, / our fathers have declared to us, / The deeds you did in their days, / in days of old: / How with your own hand you rooted out / the nations and planted them; / you smashed the peoples, but for them you made room. / For not with their own sword did they conquer the land, / nor did their own arm make them victorious, / But it was your arm and your right hand / and the light of your countenance, in your love for them. / You are my king and my God, / who bestowed victories on Jacob. / Our foes through you we struck down; / through your name we trampled down our adversaries. / For not in my bow did I trust, / nor did my sword save me; / But you saved us from our foes, / and those who hated us you put to shame. / In God we gloried day by day; / your name we praised always. / Yet now you have cast us off and put us in disgrace, / and you go not forth with our armies. / You have let us be driven back by our foes; / those who hated us plundered us at will. / You marked us out as sheep to be slaughtered; / among the nations you scattered us. / You sold your people for no great price; / you made no profit from the sale of them. / You made us the reproach of our neighbors, / the mockery and the scorn of those around us. / You made us a byword among the nations, / a laughingstock among the peoples. / All the day my disgrace is before me, / and shame covers my face / At the voice of him who mocks and blasphemes, / and in the presence of the enemy and the avenger. / All this has come upon us, though we have not forgotten you, / nor have we been disloyal to your covenant; / Our hearts have not shrunk back, / nor our steps turned aside from your path, / Though you thrust us down into a place of misery / and covered us over with darkness. / If we had forgotten the name of our God / and stretched out our hands to a strange god, / Would not God have discovered this? / For he knows the secrets of the heart. / Yet for your sake we are being slain all the day; / we are looked upon as sheep to be slaughtered. / *Awake! Why are you asleep, O Lord? / Arise! Cast us not off forever! / Why do you hide your face, / forgetting our woe and our oppression? /*

*For our souls are bowed down to the dust, / our bodies are pressed to the earth. / Arise, help us! / Redeem us for your kindness' sake.* (Ps 44)

**Community Prayer.** *The favors of the Lord I will sing forever; / through all generations my mouth shall proclaim your faithfulness.* / For you have said, "My kindness is established forever"; / in heaven you have confirmed your faithfulness: / "I have made a covenant with my chosen one, / I have sworn to David my servant: / Forever will I confirm your posterity / and establish your throne for all generations." / The heavens proclaim your wonders, O Lord, / and your faithfulness, in the assembly of the holy ones. / For who in the skies can rank with the Lord? / Who is like the Lord among the sons of God? / God is terrible in the council of the holy ones; / he is great and awesome beyond all round about him. / O Lord, God of hosts, who is like you? / Mighty are you, O Lord, and your faithfulness surrounds you. / You rule over the surging of the sea; / you still the swelling of its waves. / You have crushed Rahab with a mortal blow; / with your strong arm you have scattered your enemies. / Yours are the heavens, and yours is the earth; / the world and its fullness you have founded; / North and south you created; / Tabor and Hermon rejoice at your name. / Yours is a mighty arm; / strong is your hand, exalted your right hand. / Justice and judgment are the foundation of your throne; / kindness and truth go before you. / Happy the people who know the joyful shout; / in the light of your countenance, O Lord, they walk. / At your name they rejoice all the day, / and through your justice they are exalted. / For you are the splendor of their strength, / and by your favor our horn is exalted. / For to the Lord belongs our shield, / and to the Holy One of Israel, our king. / Once you spoke in a vision, / and to your faithful ones you said: / "On a champion I have placed a crown; / over the people I have set a youth. / I have found David, my servant; / with my holy oil I have anointed him, / That my hand may be always with him, / and that my arm may make him strong. / No enemy shall deceive him, / nor shall the wicked afflict him. / But I will crush his foes before him / and those who hate him I will smite. / My faithfulness and my kindness shall be with him, / and through my name shall his horn be exalted. / I will set his hand upon the sea, / his right hand upon the rivers. / He shall say of me, 'You are my father, / my God, the rock, my savior.' / And I will make him the first-born, / highest of the kings of the earth. / Forever I will maintain my kindness toward him, / and my covenant with him stands firm. / I will make his posterity endure forever / and his throne as the days of heaven. / If his sons forsake my law / and walk not according to my ordinances, / If they violate my statutes / and keep not my commands, / I will punish their crime with a rod / and their guilt with stripes. / Yet my kindness I will not take from him, / nor will I belie my faithfulness. / I will not violate my covenant; / the promise of my lips I will not alter. / Once, by my holiness, have I sworn; / I will not be false to David. / His posterity shall continue forever, / and his throne shall be like the sun before me; / Like the moon, which remains forever— / a faithful witness in the sky." / Yet you have rejected and spurned / and been enraged at your anointed. / You have renounced the covenant with your servant, / and defiled his crown in the dust. / You have broken down all his walls; / you have laid his strongholds in ruins. / All who pass by the way have plundered him; / he is made the reproach of his neighbors. / You have exalted the right hands of his foes, / you have gladdened all his enemies. / You have turned back his sharp sword / and have not sustained him in battle. / You have deprived him of his luster / and hurled his throne to the ground. / You have shortened the days of his youth; / you have covered him with shame. / *How long, O Lord? Will you hide yourself forever? / Will your wrath burn like fire? / Remember how short my life is; / how frail you created all the children of men! / What man shall live, and not see death, / but deliver himself from the power of the nether world? / Where are your ancient favors, O Lord, / which you pledged to David by your faithfulness? / Remember, O Lord, the insults to your servants: / I bear in my bosom all the accusations of the nations / With which your enemies have reviled, O Lord, / with which they have reviled your anointed on his way! / Blessed be the Lord forever. / Amen, and amen! (Ps 89)

**Plea for Mercy.** *To you I lift up my eyes / who are enthroned in heaven.* / Behold, as the eyes of servants / are on the hands of their masters, / As the eyes of a maid / are on the hands of her mistress, / So are our eyes on the Lord, our God, / till he have pity on us. / Have pity on us, O Lord, have pity on us, / for we are more than sated with contempt; / Our souls are more than sated / with the mockery of the arrogant, / with the contempt of the proud. (Ps 123)

**Prayer for Relief.** Much have they oppressed me from my youth, / let Israel say, / Much have they oppressed me from my youth; / yet they have not prevailed against me. / Upon my back the plowers plowed; / long did they make their furrows. / But the just Lord has severed / the cords of the wicked. / May all be put to shame and fall back that hate Zion. / May they be like grass on the housetops, / which withers before it is plucked; / With which the reaper fills not his hand, / nor the gatherer of sheaves his arms; / And those that pass by say not, / "*The blessing of the Lord be upon you! / We bless you in the name of the Lord!*" (Ps 129)

## 28. To Acknowledge Our Father as Lord

What a radical departure Jesus made from the old Jewish concept of God! Jesus taught us that God is our Father. He is our loving, kind, gracious, compassionate *Abba*. He adopted us as his sons and daughters. He said so himself: "I will dwell with them and walk among them. I will be their God and they shall be my people. . . . I will welcome you and be a father to you and you will be my sons and daughters" (2 Cor 6:16, 18).

**The Lord Is King.** Let the heavens be glad and the earth rejoice; / let them say among the nations: The Lord is king. / Let the sea and what fills it resound; / let the plains rejoice and all that is in them! / Then shall all the trees of the forest exult / before the Lord, for he comes: / he comes to rule the earth.

Give thanks to the Lord, for he is good, / for his kindness endures forever; / And say, "Save us, O God, our savior, / gather us and deliver us from the nations, / That we may give thanks to your holy name / and glory in praising you." / Blessed be the Lord, the God of Israel, through all eternity! / Let all the people say, Amen! Alleluia! (1 Chr 16:31-36)

**No One like the Lord.** No one is like you, O Lord, / great are you, / great and mighty is your name. (Jer 10:6)

**King of Heaven.** I now praise and exalt and glorify the King of heaven, because all his works are right and his ways just; and those who walk in pride he is able to humble. (Dn 4:34)

*Abba,* **Father.** *"Abba* (O Father), you have the power to do all things." (Mk 14:36a)

**The Father's Glory.** "My soul is troubled now, / yet what should I say— / Father, save me from this hour? / But it was for this that I came to this hour. / Father, glorify your name!" (Jn 12:27-28a)

**All Glory.** To him whose power now at work in us can do immeasurably more than we ask or imagine—to him be glory in the church and in Christ Jesus through all generations, world without end. Amen. (Eph 3:20-21)

**King of Glory.** *The Lord's are the earth and its fullness; / the world and those who dwell in it.* / For he founded it upon the seas / and established it upon the rivers. / Who can ascend the mountain of the Lord? / or who may stand in his holy place? / He whose hands are sinless, whose heart is clean, / who desires not what is vain, / nor swears deceitfully to his neighbor. / He shall receive a blessing from the Lord, / a reward from God his savior. / Such is the race that seeks for him, / that seeks the face of the God of Jacob. / Lift up, O gates, your lintels; / reach up, you ancient portals, / that the king of glory may come in! / Who is this king of glory? / The Lord, strong and mighty, / the Lord, mighty in battle. / *Lift up, O gates, your lintels; / reach up, you ancient portals, / that the king of glory may come in! / Who is this king of glory? / The Lord of hosts; he is the king of glory.* (Ps 24)

**He Is Supreme.** *All you peoples, clap your hands, / shout to God with cries of gladness, / For the Lord, the Most High, the awesome, / is the great king over all the earth.* / He brings peoples under us; / nations under our feet. / He chooses for us our inheritance, / the glory of Jacob, whom he loves. / God mounts his throne amid shouts of joy; / the Lord, amid trumpet blasts. / Sing praise to God, sing praise; / sing praise to our king, sing praise. / *For king of all the earth is God; / sing hymns of praise. / God reigns over the nations, / God sits upon his holy throne.* / The princes of the peoples are gathered together / with the people of the God of Abraham. / For God's are the guardians of the earth; / he is supreme. (Ps 47)

**His Reign Is Eternal.** *The Lord is king, in splendor robed; / robed is the Lord and girt about with strength; / And he has made the world firm, / not to be moved. / Your throne stands firm from of old; / from everlasting you are, O Lord.* / The floods lift up, O Lord, / the floods lift up their voice; / the floods lift up their tumult. / More powerful than the roar of many waters, / more powerful than the breakers of the sea—/ powerful on high is the Lord. / Your decrees are worthy of trust indeed: / holiness befits your house, / O Lord, for length of days. (Ps 93)

**King of the Universe.** Sing to the Lord a new song; / sing to the Lord, all you lands. / Sing to the Lord; bless his name; / announce his salvation, day after day. / Tell his glory among the nations; / among all peoples, his wondrous deeds. / *For great is the Lord and highly to be praised; / awesome is he, beyond all gods. / For all the gods of the nations are things of nought, / but the Lord made the heavens. / Splendor and majesty go before him; / praise and grandeur are in his sanctuary.* / Give to the Lord, you families of nations, / give to the Lord glory and praise; / give to the Lord the glory due his name! / Bring gifts, and enter his courts; / worship the Lord in holy attire. / Tremble before him, all the earth; / say among the nations: The Lord is king. / He has made the world firm, not to be moved; / he governs the peoples with equity. / Let the heavens be glad and the earth rejoice; / let the sea and what fills it resound; / let the plains be joyful and all that is in them! / Then shall all the trees of the forest exult / before the Lord, for he comes; / for he comes to rule the earth. / He shall rule the world with justice / and the peoples with his constancy. (Ps 96)

**Our King Is Holy.** *The Lord is king; the peoples tremble; / he is throned upon the cherubim; the earth quakes. / The Lord in Zion is great, / he is high above all the peoples. / Let them praise your great and awesome name; holy is he!* / The King in his might loves justice; / you have established equity; / justice and judgment in Jacob you have wrought. / Extol the Lord, our God, / and worship at his footstool; / holy is he! / Moses and Aaron were among his priests, / and Samuel, among those who called upon his name; / they called upon the Lord, and he answered them. / From the pillar of cloud he spoke to them; / they heard his decrees and the law he gave them. / O Lord, our God, you answered them; / a forgiving God you were to them, / though requiting their misdeeds. / *Extol the Lord, our God,* / *and worship at his holy mountain;* / *for holy is the Lord, our God.* (Ps 99)

## 29. To Rejoice in God's Judgments

In spite of the fact that Jesus said, "Do not judge, and you will not be judged" (Lk 6:37), we have a strong tendency to sit in judgment on others. We are playing God, since only God can know the human heart. Jeremiah gave us some words of wisdom: "I, the Lord, alone probe the mind / and test the heart, / to reward everyone according to his ways, / according to the merit of his deeds" (Jer 17:10).

**Just Judge.** You would be in the right, O Lord, / if I should dispute with you; / even so, I must discuss the case with you. / Why does the way of the godless prosper, / why live all the treacherous in contentment? / You planted them; they have taken root, / they keep on growing and bearing fruit. / You are upon their lips, / but far from their inmost thoughts. / You, O Lord, know me, you see me, / you have found that at heart I am with you. / Pick them out like sheep for the slaughter, / set them apart for the day of carnage. / How long must the earth mourn, / the green of the whole countryside wither? / For the wickedness of those who dwell in it / beasts and birds disappear, / because they say, "God does not see our ways."

If running against men has wearied you, / how will you race against horses? / And if in a land of peace you fall headlong, / what will you do in the thickets of the Jordan? . . . But, you, O Lord of hosts, O just Judge, / searcher of mind and heart, / Let me witness the vengeance you take on them, / for to you I have entrusted my cause! (Jer 12:1-5, 20)

**Like Spring Rain.** "Let us know, let us strive to know the Lord; / as certain as the dawn is his coming, / and his judgment shines forth like the light of day! / He will come to us like the rain, / like spring rain that waters the earth." (Hos 6:3)

**True and Just.** "You are just, O Holy One / who is and who was, / in passing this sentence!" . . . "Yes, Lord God Almighty, / your judgments are true and just!" (Rv 16:5b, 7b)

**His Judgments Are True.** "Alleluia! / Salvation, glory and might belong to our God, / for his judgments are true and just! / He has condemned the great harlot / who corrupted the earth with her harlotry. / He has avenged the blood of his servants / which was shed by her hand." (Rv 19:1b-2)

**Honest Appeal.** O Lord, my God, in you I take refuge; / save me from all my pursuers and rescue me, / Lest I become like the lion's prey, / to be torn to pieces, with no one to rescue me. / O Lord, my God, if I am at fault in this, / if there is guilt on my hands, / if I have repaid my friend with evil, / I who spared those who without cause were my foes— / Let the enemy pursue and overtake me; / let him trample my life to the ground, / and lay my glory in the dust. / Rise up, O Lord, in your anger; / rise against the fury of my foes; / wake to the judgment you have decreed. / Let the assembly of the peoples surround you; / above them on high be enthroned. / [The Lord judges the nations.] / Do me justice, O Lord, because I am just, and because of the innocence that is mine. / Let the malice of the wicked come to an end, / but sustain the just, / O searcher of heart and soul, O just God. / *A shield before me is God, / who saves the upright of heart; / A just judge is God,* / a God who punishes day by day. / Unless they be converted, God will sharpen his sword; / he will bend and aim his bow, / Prepare his deadly weapons against them, / and use fiery darts for arrows. / He who conceived iniquity and was pregnant with mischief, / brings forth failure. / He has opened a hole, he has dug it deep, / but he falls into the pit which he has made. / His mischief shall recoil upon his own head; / upon the crown of his head his violence shall rebound. / *I will give thanks to the Lord for his justice, / and sing praise to the name of the Lord Most High.* (Ps 7)

**God Is the Judge.** We give you thanks, O God, we give thanks, / and we invoke your name; we declare your wondrous deeds. / *"When I seize the appointed time, / I will judge with equity. /* Though the earth and all who dwell in it quake, / I have set firm its pillars. / I say to the boastful: Boast not; / and to the wicked: Lift not up your horns." /

Lift not up your horns against the Most High; / speak not haughtily against the Rock. / For neither from the east nor from the west, / neither from the desert nor from the mountains— / *But God is the judge; / one he brings low; another he lifts up.* / For a cup is in the Lord's hand, / full of spiced and foaming wine, / And he pours out from it; even to the dregs they shall drain it; / all the wicked of the earth shall drink. / But as for me, I will exult forever; / I will sing praise to the God of Jacob. / And I will break off the horns of all the wicked; / the horns of the just shall be lifted up. (Ps 75)

**Unjust Judges.** God arises in the divine assembly; / he judges in the midst of the gods. / "How long will you judge unjustly / and favor the cause of the wicked? / *Defend the lowly and the fatherless; / render justice to the afflicted and the destitute. / Rescue the lowly and the poor; / from the hand of the wicked deliver them.* / "They know not, neither do they understand; / they go about in darkness; / all the foundations of the earth are shaken. / I said: You are gods, / all of you sons of the Most High; / Yet like men you shall die, / and fall like any prince." / Rise, O God; judge the earth, / for yours are all the nations. (Ps 82)

**Divine Justice.** God of vengeance, Lord, / God of vengeance, show yourself. / Rise up, judge of the earth; / render their deserts to the proud. / How long, O Lord, shall the wicked, / how long shall the wicked glory, / Mouthing insolent speeches, / boasting, all the evildoers? / Your people, O Lord, they trample down, / your inheritance they afflict. / Widow and stranger they slay, / the fatherless they murder, / And they say, "The Lord sees not; / the God of Jacob perceives not." / *Understand, you senseless ones among the people; / and, you fools, when will you be wise? / Shall he who shaped the ear not hear? / or he who formed the eye not see? / Shall he who instructs nations not chastise, / he who teaches men knowledge? / The Lord knows the thoughts of men, / and that they are vain.* / Happy the man whom you instruct, O Lord, / whom by your law you teach, / Giving him rest from evil days, / till the pit be dug for the wicked. / For the Lord will not cast off his people, / nor abandon his inheritance; / But judgment shall again be with justice, / and all the upright of heart shall follow it. / Who will rise up for me against the wicked? / Who will stand by me against the evildoers? / Were not the Lord my help, / I would soon dwell in the silent grave. / When I say, "My foot is slipping," / your kindness, O Lord, sustains me; / When cares abound within me, / your comfort gladdens my soul. / How could the tribunal of wickedness be leagued with you, / which creates burdens in the guise of law? / Though they attack the life of the just / and condemn innocent blood, / Yet the Lord is my stronghold, / and my God the rock of my refuge. / And he will requite them for their evildoing, / and for their wickedness he will destroy them; / the Lord, our God, will destroy them. (Ps 94)

## 30. To Proclaim Jesus as King

The kingdom that Jesus came to establish is not the reign of an autocratic despot but rather a kingdom governed by love. Jesus himself said, "My kingdom does not belong to this world" (Jn 18:36). The prophecies are rich in proclaiming Jesus as king. The Magi asked Herod, "Where is the newborn king of the Jews?" (Mt 2:2). The prophet envisions Jesus as a humble, gentle king: "See, your king shall come to you; / a just savior is he, / Meek, and riding on an ass, / on a colt, the foal of an ass" (Zec 9:9).

**He Comes as King.** "Blessed is he who comes as king / in the name of the Lord! / Peace in heaven / and glory in the highest!" (Lk 19:38)

**Resplendent Reign.** "Jesus, remember me when you enter upon your reign." (Lk 23:42)

**Jesus Is Lord.** Though he was in the form of God, / he did not deem equality with God / something to be grasped at. / Rather, he emptied himself / and took the form of a slave, / being born in the likeness of men. / He was known to be of human estate, / and it was thus that he humbled himself, / obediently accepting even death, / death on a cross! / Because of this, / God highly exalted him / and bestowed on him the name / above every other name, / So that at Jesus' name / every knee must bend / in the heavens, on the earth, / and under the earth, / and every tongue proclaim / to the glory of God the Father: / JESUS CHRIST IS LORD! (Phil 2:6-11)

**Praise Our King.** "We praise you, the Lord God Almighty, / who is and who was. / You have assumed your great power, / you have begun your reign." (Rv 11:17)

**Brilliant White.** "Alleluia! / The Lord is king, / our God, the Almighty! / Let us rejoice and be glad, / and give him glory! / For this is the wedding day of the Lamb; / his bride has prepared herself for the wedding. / She has been given a dress to wear / made of finest linen, brilliant white." (Rv 19:6b-8)

**Kingdom of Love.** Why do the nations rage / and the peoples utter folly? / The kings of the earth rise up, / and the princes conspire together / against the Lord and against his anointed: / "Let us break their fetters / and cast their bonds from us!" / He who is throned in heaven laughs; / the Lord derides them. / Then in anger he speaks to them; / he terrifies them in his wrath: / "I myself have set up my king / on Zion, my holy mountain." / I will proclaim the decree of the Lord: / *The Lord said to me, "You are my son; / this day I have begotten you. / Ask of me and I will give you / the nations for an inheritance / and the ends of the earth for your possession. / You shall rule them with an iron rod; / you shall shatter them like an earthen dish." / And now, O kings, give heed; / take warning, you rulers of the earth. / Serve the Lord with fear, and rejoice before him; / with trembling pay homage to him, / Lest he be angry and you perish from the way, / when his anger blazes suddenly. / Happy are all who take refuge in him! (Ps 2)

**Royal Bridegroom.** *My heart overflows with a goodly theme; / as I sing my ode to the king, / my tongue is nimble as the pen of a skillful scribe. / Fairer in beauty are you than the sons of men; / grace is poured out upon your lips; / thus God has blessed you forever. /* Gird your sword upon your thigh, O mighty one! / In your spendor and your majesty ride on triumphant / In the cause of truth and for the sake of justice; / and may your right hand show you wondrous deeds. / Your arrows are sharp; peoples are subject to you; / the king's enemies lose heart. / Your throne, O God, stands forever and ever; / a tempered rod is your royal scepter. / You love justice and hate wickedness; / therefore God, your God, has anointed you / with the oil of gladness above your fellow kings. / With myrrh and aloes and cassia your robes are fragrant; / from ivory palaces string music brings you joy. / The daughters of kings come to meet you; / the queen takes her place at your right hand in gold of Ophir. / Hear, O daughter, and see; turn your ear, / forget your people and your father's house. / So shall the king desire your beauty; / for he is your lord, and you must worship him. / And the city of Tyre is here with gifts: / the rich among the people seek your favor. / All glorious is the king's daughter as she enters; / her raiment is threaded with spun gold. / In embroidered apparel she is borne in to the king; / behind her the virgins of her train are brought to you. / They are borne in with gladness and joy; / they enter the palace of the king. / The place of your fathers your sons shall have; / you shall make them princes through all the land. / I will make your name memorable through all generations; / therefore shall nations praise you forever and ever. (Ps 45)

**My King.** O God, with your judgment endow the king, / and with your justice, the king's son; / He shall govern your people with justice / and your afflicted ones with judgment. / The mountains shall yield peace for the people, / and the hills justice. / He shall defend the afflicted among the people, / save the children of the poor, / and crush the oppressor. / May he endure as long as the sun, / and like the moon through all generations. / He shall be like rain coming down on the meadow, / like showers watering the earth. / Justice shall flower in his days, / and profound peace, till the moon be no more. / May he rule from sea to sea, / and from the River to the ends of the earth. / His foes shall bow before him, / and his enemies shall lick the dust. / The kings of Tarshish and the Isles shall offer gifts; / the kings of Arabia and Seba shall bring tribute. / All kings shall pay him homage, / all nations shall serve him. / For he shall rescue the poor man when he cries out, / and the afflicted when he has no one to help him. / He shall have pity for the lowly and the poor; / the lives of the poor he shall save. / From fraud and violence he shall redeem them, / and precious shall their blood be in his sight. / May he live to be given the gold of Arabia, / and to be prayed for continually; / day by day shall they bless him. / May there be an abundance of grain upon the earth; / on the tops of the mountains the crops shall rustle like Lebanon; / the city dwellers shall flourish like the verdure of the fields. / *May his name be blessed forever; / as long as the sun his name shall remain. / In him shall all the tribes of the earth be blessed; / all the nations shall proclaim his happiness.* / Blessed be the Lord, the God of Israel, / who alone does wondrous deeds. / And blessed forever be his glorious name; / may the whole earth be filled with his glory. / Amen. Amen. / The prayers of David the son of Jesse are ended. (Ps 72)

**King and Savior.** Sing to the Lord a new song, / for he has done wondrous deeds; / His right hand has won victory for him, / his holy arm. / The Lord has made his salvation known: / in the sight of the nations he has revealed his justice. / He has remembered his kindness and his faithfulness / toward the house of Israel. / All the ends of the earth have seen / the salvation by our God. / *Sing joyfully to the Lord, all you lands; / break into song; sing praise. / Sing praise to the Lord with the harp, / with the harp and melodious song. / With trumpets and the sound of the horn / sing joyfully before the King, the Lord.* / Let the sea and what fills it resound, / the world and those who dwell in it; / Let the rivers clap their hands, the mountains shout with them for joy / Before the Lord, for he comes, / for he comes to rule the earth; / He will rule the world with justice / and the peoples with equity. (Ps 98)

## 31. *To Acclaim Jesus as Savior*

When sin entered the world, God did not write off the human race, as well he might have. The Garden of Eden was a sad story with a happy ending, because our merciful Father promised us a redeemer. At his birth Jesus was announced as our redeemer: "This day in David's city a savior has been born to you, the Messiah and Lord" (Lk 2:11). Peter gave no room for equivocation: "There is no salvation in anyone else, for there is no other name in the whole world given to men by which we are to be saved" (Acts 4:12).

**Source of Strength.** "My strength and my courage is the Lord, / and he has been my savior. / He is my God, I praise him; / the God of my father, I extol him." (Ex 15:2)

**Chosen by God.** Praised be the God and Father of our Lord Jesus Christ, who has bestowed on us in Christ every spiritual blessing in the heavens! God chose us in him before the world began, to be holy and blameless in his sight, to be full of love; he likewise predestined us through Christ Jesus to be his adopted sons—such was his will and pleasure—that all might praise the glorious favor he has bestowed on us in his beloved.

It is in Christ and through his blood that we have been redeemed and our sins forgiven, so immeasurably generous is God's favor to us. God has given us the wisdom to understand fully the mystery, the plan he was pleased to decree in Christ, to be carried out in the fullness of time: namely, to bring all things in the heavens and on earth into one under Christ's headship. (Eph 1:3-10)

**Majestic Savior.** Glory be to this only God our savior, through Jesus Christ our Lord. Majesty, too, be his, might and power from ages past, now and for ages to come. Amen. (Jude 25)

**Purchased for God.** "Worthy are you to receive the scroll / and break open its seals, / for you were slain. / With your blood you purchased for God / men of every race and tongue, / of every people and nation. / You made of them a kingdom, / and priests to serve our God, / and they shall reign on the earth." (Rv 5:9-10)

**Lamb of Glory.** "Worthy is the Lamb that was slain / to receive power and riches, wisdom and strength, / honor and glory and praise! ... To the One seated on the throne, and to the Lamb, / be praise and honor, glory and might, / forever and ever!" (Rv 5:12b-13b)

**His Dying Prayer.** My God, my God, why have you forsaken me, / far from my prayer, from the words of my cry? / O my God, I cry out by day, and you answer not; / by night, and there is no relief for me. / Yet you are enthroned in the holy place, / O glory of Israel! / In you our fathers trusted; / they trusted, and you delivered them. / To you they cried, and they escaped; / in you they trusted, and they were not put to shame. / But I am a worm, not a man; / the scorn of men, despised by the people. / All who see me scoff at me; / they mock me with parted lips, they wag their heads: / "He relied on the Lord; let him deliver him, / let him rescue him, if he loves him." / You have been my guide since I was first formed, / my security at my mother's breast. / To you I was committed at birth, / From my mother's womb you are my God. / Be not far from me, for I am in distress; / be near, for I have no one to help me. / Many bullocks surround me; / the strong bulls of Bashan encircle me. / They open their mouths against me / like ravening and roaring lions. / I am like water poured out; / all my bones are racked. / My heart has become like wax / melting away within my bosom. / My throat is dried up like baked clay, / my tongue cleaves to my jaws; / to the dust of death you have brought me down. / Indeed, many dogs surround me, / a pack of evildoers closes in upon me; / They have pierced my hands and my feet; / I can count all my bones. / They look on and gloat over me; / they divide my garments among them, / and for my vesture they cast lots. / But you, O Lord, be not far from me; / O my help, hasten to aid me. / Rescue my soul from the

sword, / my loneliness from the grip of the dog. / Save
me from the lion's mouth; / from the horns of the wild
bulls, my wretched life. / *I will proclaim your name to my
brethren; / in the midst of the assembly I will praise you:* /
"You who fear the Lord, praise him; / all you descendants of Jacob, give glory to him; / revere him, all you
descendants of Israel! / For he has not spurned nor
disdained / the wretched man in his misery, / Nor did he
turn his face away from him, / but when he cried out to
him, he heard him." / So by your gift will I utter praise in
the vast assembly; / I will fulfill my vows before those
who fear him. / The lowly shall eat their fill; / they who
seek the Lord shall praise him: / "May your hearts be ever
merry!" / All the ends of the earth / shall remember and
turn to the Lord; / All the families of the nations / shall
bow down before him. / For dominion is the Lord's, /
and he rules the nations. / *To him alone shall bow down / all
who sleep in the earth; / Before him shall bend / all who go
down into the dust. / And to him my soul shall live; / my
descendants shall serve him.* / Let the coming generation be
told of the Lord / that they may proclaim to a people yet
to be born / the justice he has shown. (Ps 22)

**Cry of Anguish.** Save me, O God, / for the waters
threaten my life; / I am sunk in the abysmal swamp /
where there is no foothold; / I have reached the watery
depths; / the flood overwhelms me. / I am wearied with
calling, / my throat is parched; / My eyes have failed /
with looking for my God. / Those outnumber the hairs
of my head / who hate me without cause. / Too many for
my strength / are they who wrongfully are my enemies. /
Must I restore what I did not steal? / O God, you know
my folly, / and my faults are not hid from you. / Let not

those who wait for you be put to shame through me, / O Lord, God of hosts. / Let not those who seek you blush for me, / O God of Israel, / Since for your sake I bear insult, / and shame covers my face. / I have become an outcast to my brothers, / a stranger to my mother's sons, / Because zeal for your house consumes me, / and the insults of those who blaspheme you fall upon me. / I humbled myself with fasting, / and this was made a reproach to me. / I made sackcloth my garment, / and I became a byword for them. / They who sit at the gate gossip about me, / and drunkards make me the butt of their songs. / But I pray to you, O Lord, / for the time of your favor, O God! / In your great kindness answer me / with your constant help. / Rescue me out of the mire; / may I not sink! / may I be rescued from my foes, / and from the watery depths. / Let not the flood-waters overwhelm me, / nor the abyss swallow me up, / nor the pit close its mouth over me. / Answer me, O Lord, for bounteous is your kindness; / in your great mercy turn toward me. / Hide not your face from your servant; / in my distress, make haste to answer me. / *Come and ransom my life; / as an answer for my enemies, redeem me.* / You know my reproach, my shame and my ignominy: / before you are all my foes. / Insult has broken my heart, and I am weak, / I looked for sympathy, but there was none; / for comforters, and I found none. / Rather they put gall in my food, / and in my thirst they gave me vinegar to drink. / Let their own table be a snare before them, / and a net for their friends. / Let their eyes grow dim so that they cannot see, / and keep their back always feeble. / Pour out your wrath upon them; / let the fury of your anger overtake them. / Let their encampment become desolate;

/ in their tents let there be no one to dwell. / For they kept after him whom you smote, / and added to the pain of him you wounded. / Heap guilt upon their guilt, / and let them not attain to your reward. / May they be erased from the book of the living, / and not be recorded with the just! / *But I am afflicted and in pain; / let your saving help, O God, protect me.* / I will praise the name of God in song, / and I will glorify him with thanksgiving; / This will please the Lord more than oxen / or bullocks with horns and divided hooves: / *"See, you lowly ones, and be glad; / you who seek God, may your hearts be merry! / For the Lord hears the poor, / and his own who are in bonds he spurns not.* / Let the heavens and the earth praise him, / the seas and whatever moves in them!" / For God will save Zion / and rebuild the cities of Judah. / They shall dwell in the land and own it, / and the descendants of his servants shall inherit it, / and those who love his name shall inhabit it. (Ps 69)

**A Priest Forever.** The Lord said to my Lord: "Sit at my right hand / till I make your enemies your footstool." / The scepter of your power the Lord will stretch forth from Zion: / "Rule in the midst of your enemies. / *Yours is princely power in the day of your birth, in holy splendor; / before the daystar, like the dew, I have begotten you."* / The Lord has sworn, and he will not repent: / *"You are a priest forever, according to the order of Melchizedek."* / The Lord is at your right hand; / he will crush kings on the day of his wrath. / He will do judgment on the nations, heaping up corpses; / he will crush heads over the wide earth. / From the brook by the wayside he will drink; / therefore will he lift up his head. (Ps 110)

## 32. *To Appreciate the Eucharist*

Each time we offer the Eucharist we enter into God's "eternal now," where Jesus is forever offering himself with us and for us. The Eucharist is a unifying sacrament, since every baptized person makes the corporate offering with us. St. Paul made it unmistakably clear: "Is not the cup of blessing we bless a sharing in the blood of Christ? And is not the bread we break a sharing in the body of Christ? Because the loaf of bread is one, we, many though we are, are one body, for we all partake of the one loaf" (1 Cor 10:16-17).

**Bread of Heaven.** "Happy is he who eats bread in the kingdom of God." (Lk 14:15)

**Give Us This Bread.** "Sir, give us this bread always." (Jn 6:34)

**No One Else.** "Lord, to whom shall we go? You have the words of eternal life. We have come to believe; we are convinced that you are God's holy one." (Jn 6:68b-69)

**Eucharistic Hymn.** Shout joyfully to God, all you on earth; / sing praise to the glory of his name; / proclaim his glorious praise. / Say to God, "How tremendous are your deeds! / for your great strength your enemies fawn upon you. / Let all on earth worship and sing praise to you, / sing praise to your name!" / Come and see the works of God, / his tremendous deeds among men. / He has changed the sea into dry land; / through the river they passed on foot; / therefore let us rejoice in him. / He rules by his might forever; / his eyes watch the nations; / rebels may not exalt themselves. / *Bless our God, you peoples, / loudly sound his praise; / He has given life to our souls, / and has not let our feet slip.* / For you have tested us, O God! / You have tried us as silver is tried by fire; / You have brought us into a snare; / you laid a heavy burden on our backs. / You let men ride over our heads; / we went through fire and water, / but you have led us out to refreshment. / I will bring holocausts to your house; / to you I will fulfill the vows / Which my lips uttered / and my words promised in my distress. / Holocausts of fatlings I will offer you, / with burnt offerings of rams; / I will sacrifice oxen and goats. / Hear now, all you who fear God, while I declare / what he has done for me. / When I appealed to him in words, / praise was on the tip of my tongue. / Were I to cherish wickedness in my heart, / the Lord would not hear; / But God has heard; / he has hearkened to the sound of my prayer. / Blessed be God who refused me not / my prayer or his kindness! (Ps 66)

**Bread of the Mighty.** Hearken, my people, to my teaching; / incline your ears to the words of my mouth. / I will open my mouth in a parable, / I will utter mysteries from of old. / What we have heard and know, / and what our fathers have declared to us, / We will not hide from their sons; / we will declare to the generation to come / The glorious deeds of the Lord and his strength / and the wonders that he wrought. / He set it up as a decree in Jacob, / and established it as a law in Israel, / That what he commanded our fathers / they should make known to their sons; / So that the generation to come might know, / their sons yet to be born, / That they too may rise and declare to their sons / that they should put their hope in God, / And not forget the deeds of God / but keep his commands, / And not be like their fathers, / a generation wayward and rebellious, / A generation that kept not its heart steadfast / nor its spirit faithful toward God. / The sons of Ephraim, ordered ranks of bowmen, / retreated in the day of battle. / They kept not the covenant with God; / according to his law they would not walk; / And they forgot his deeds, / the wonders he had shown them. / Before their fathers he did wondrous things, / in the land of Egypt, in the plain of Zoan. / He cleft the sea and brought them through, / and he made the waters stand as in a mound. / He led them with a cloud by day, / and all night with a glow of fire. / He cleft the rocks in the desert / and gave them water in copious floods. / He made streams flow from the crag / and brought the waters forth in rivers. / But they sinned yet more against him, / rebelling against the Most High in the wasteland, / And they tempted God in their hearts / by demanding the food they craved. / Yes, they spoke against God, saying, / "Can God spread a table in the desert? / For when he struck the rock, waters gushed forth, / and the streams overflowed; / Can he also give bread / and provide meat for his people?" / Then the Lord heard and was enraged; / and fire blazed up against Jacob, / and anger rose against Israel, / Because they believed not God / nor trusted in his help. / *Yet he commanded the skies above / and the doors of heaven he opened; / He rained manna upon them for food / and gave them heavenly bread. / The bread of the mighty was eaten by men; / even a surfeit of provisions he sent them.* / He stirred up the east wind in the heavens, / and by his power brought on the south wind. / And he rained meat upon them like dust, / and, like the sand of the sea, winged fowl, / Which fell in the midst of their camp /

round about their tents. / So they ate and were wholly surfeited; / he had brought them what they craved. / They had not given over their craving, / and their food was still in their mouths, / When the anger of God rose against them / and slew their best men, / and laid low the young men of Israel. / Yet for all this they sinned still more / and believed not in his wonders. / Therefore he quickly ended their days / and their years with sudden destruction. / While he slew them they sought him / and inquired after God again, / Remembering that God was their rock / and the Most High God, their redeemer. / But they flattered him with their mouths / and lied to him with their tongues, / Though their hearts were not steadfast toward him, / nor were they faithful to his covenant. / Yet he, being merciful, forgave their sin / and destroyed them not; / Often he turned back his anger / and let none of his wrath be roused. / He remembered that they were flesh, / a passing breath that returns not. / How often they rebelled against him in the desert / and grieved him in the wilderness! / Again and again they tempted God / and provoked the Holy One of Israel. / They remembered not his hand / nor the day he delivered them from the foe, / When he wrought his signs in Egypt / and his marvels in the plain of Zoan, / And changed into blood their streams— / their running water, so that they could not drink; / He sent among them flies that devoured them / and frogs that destroyed them. / He gave their harvest to the caterpillar, / the fruits of their toil to the locust. / He killed their vines with hail / and their sycamores with frost. / He gave over to the hail their beasts / and their flocks to the lightning. / He loosed against them his fierce anger, / wrath and fury and strife, / a detachment of messengers of doom. / When he measured the course of his anger / he spared them not from death, / and delivered their beasts to the plague. / He smote every first-born in Egypt, / the first fruits of manhood in the tents of Ham; / But his people he led forth like sheep / and guided them like a herd in the desert. / He led them on secure and unafraid, / while he covered their enemies with the sea. / And he brought them to his holy land, / to the mountains his right hand had won. / And he drove out nations before them; / he distributed their inheritance by lot, / and settled the tribes of Israel in their tents. / But they tempted and rebelled against God the Most High, / and kept not his decrees. / They turned back and were faithless like their fathers; / they recoiled like a treacherous bow. / They angered him with their high places / and with their idols roused his jealousy. / God heard and was enraged / and utterly rejected Israel. / And he forsook the tabernacle in Shiloh, / the tent where he dwelt among men. / And he surrendered his strength into captivity, / his glory into the hands of the foe. / He abandoned his people to the sword / and was enraged against his inheritance. / Fire consumed their young men, / and their maidens were not betrothed. / Their priests fell by the sword, / and their widows sang no dirges. / Then the Lord awoke, as wakes from sleep / a champion overcome with wine; / And he put his foes to flight / and cast them into everlasting disgrace. / And he rejected the tent of Joseph, / and the tribe of Ephraim he chose not; / But he chose the tribe of Judah, / Mount Zion which he loved. / And he built his shrine like heaven, / like the earth which he founded forever. / And he chose David, his servant, / and took him from the sheepfolds; / From following the ewes he brought him / to shepherd Jacob, his people, / and Israel, his inheritance. / And he tended them with a sincere heart, / and with skillful hands he guided them. (Ps 78)

**Cup of Salvation.** I love the Lord because he has heard / my voice in supplication, / Because he has inclined his ear to me / the day I called. / The cords of death encompassed me; / the snares of the nether world seized upon me; / I fell into distress and sorrow, / And I called upon the name of the Lord, / "O Lord, save my life!" / Gracious is the Lord and just; / yes, our God is merciful. / The Lord keeps the little ones; / I was brought low, and he saved me. / Return, O my soul, to your tranquillity, / for the Lord has been good to you. / For he has freed my soul from death, / my eyes from tears, my feet from stumbling. / I shall walk before the Lord / in the lands of the living. / I believed, even when I said, / "I am greatly afflicted"; / I said in my alarm, / "No man is dependable." / *How shall I make a return to the Lord / for all the good he has done for me? / The cup of salvation I will take up, / and I will call upon the name of the Lord;* / My vows to the Lord I will pay / in the presence of all his people. / Precious in the eyes of the Lord / is the death of his faithful ones. / O Lord, I am your servant; / I am your servant, the son of your handmaid; / you have loosed my bonds. / To you will I offer sacrifice of thanksgiving, / and I will call upon the name of the Lord. / My vows to the Lord I will pay / in the presence of all his people, / In the courts of the house of the Lord, / in your midst, O Jerusalem. (Ps 116)

## 33. To Focus on Our Eternal Destiny

"Judge everything in the light of eternity" is an axiom that may at first strike us as rather negative and confining. On the other hand, it can be very positive and energizing. When we keep our focus on eternity, the rough, rocky road of life seems more negotiable, the hills not quite so hilly and the valleys not quite so deep, for they all lead to our eternal destiny of unimaginable bliss in a community of perfect love. "Father, / all those you gave me / I would have in my company / where I am, / to see this glory of mine" (Jn 17:24).

**Dew from Heaven.** "May God give to you / of the dew of the heavens / And of the fertility of the earth / abundance of grain and wine." (Gn 27:28)

**Wisdom Indispensable.** God of my fathers, Lord of mercy, / you who have made all things by your word / And in your wisdom have established man / to rule the creatures produced by you, / To govern the world in holiness and justice, / and to render judgment in integrity of heart: / Give me Wisdom, the attendant at your throne, / and reject me not from among your children; / For I am your servant, the son of your handmaid, / a man weak and short-lived / and lacking in comprehension of judgment and of laws. / Indeed, though one be perfect among the sons of men, / if Wisdom, who comes from you, be not with him, / he shall be held in no esteem. (Wis 9:1-6)

**No Victory.** "Death is swallowed up in victory." "O death, where is your victory? O death, where is your sting?" The sting of death is sin, and sin gets its power from the law. But thanks be to God who has given us the victory through our Lord Jesus Christ. (1 Cor 15:54b-57)

**Christ the Way.** May the God of our Lord Jesus Christ, the Father of glory, grant you a spirit of wisdom and insight to know him clearly. May he enlighten your innermost vision that you may know the great hope to which he has called you, the wealth of his glorious heritage to be distributed among the members of the church, and the immeasurable scope of his power in us who believe. It is like the strength he showed in raising Christ from the dead and seating him at his right hand in heaven, high above every principality, power, virtue, and domination, and every name that can be given in this age or in the age to come.

He has put all things under Christ's feet and has made him, thus exalted, head of the church, which is his body: the fullness of him who fills the universe in all its parts. (Eph 1:17-23)

**God Reveals the Way We Should Live.** Happy are they whose way is blameless, / who walk in the law of the Lord. / *Happy are they who observe his decrees, / who seek him with all their heart, / And do no wrong, but walk in his ways.* / You have commanded that your precepts / be diligently kept. / Oh, that I might be firm in the ways / of keeping your statutes! / Then should I not be put to shame / when I beheld all your commands. / I will give you thanks with an upright heart, / when I have learned your just ordinances. / I will keep your statutes; / do not utterly forsake me. / How shall a young man be faultless in his way? / By keeping to your words. / With all my heart I seek you; / let me not stray from your commands. / *Within my heart I treasure your promise, / that I may not sin against you.* / Blessed are you, O Lord; / teach me your statutes. / With my lips I declare / all the ordinances of your mouth. / In the way of your decrees I rejoice, / as much as in all riches. / I will meditate on your precepts / and consider your ways. / In your statutes I will delight; / I will not forget your words. / Be good to your servant, that I may live / and keep your words. / *Open my eyes, that I may consider / the wonders of your law.* / I am a wayfarer of earth; / hide not your commands from me. / My soul is consumed with longing / for your ordinances at all times. / You rebuke the accursed proud, / who turn away from your commands. / Take away from me reproach and contempt, / for I observe your decrees. / Though princes meet and talk against me, / your servant meditates on your statutes./ Yes, your decrees are my delight; / they are my counselors. / I lie prostrate in the dust; / give me life according to your word. / I declared my ways, and you answered me; / teach me your statutes. / Make me understand the way of your precepts, / and I will meditate on your wondrous deeds. / My soul weeps for sorrow; / strengthen me according to your words. / Remove from me the way of falsehood, / and favor me with your law. / The way of truth I have chosen; / I have set your ordinances before me. / I cling to your decrees; / O Lord, let me not be put to shame. / *I will run the way of your commands / when you give me a docile heart.* / Instruct me, O Lord, in the way of your statutes, / that I may exactly observe them. / *Give me discernment, that I may observe your law / and keep it with all my heart.* / Lead me in the path of your commands, / for in it I delight. / Incline my heart to your decrees / and not to gain. / Turn away my eyes from seeing what is vain; / by your way give me life. / Fulfill for your servant / your promise to those who fear you. / Turn away from me the reproach which I dread, / for your ordinances are good. / Behold, I long for your precepts; / in your justice give me life. / *Let your kindness come to me, O Lord, / your salvation according to your promise.* / So shall I have an answer for those who reproach me, / for I trust in your words. / Take not the word of truth from my mouth, / for in your ordinances is my hope; / And I will keep your law continually, / forever and ever. / And I will walk at liberty; / because I seek your precepts. / I will speak of your decrees before kings / without being ashamed. / And I will delight in your commands, / which I love. / And I will lift up my hands to your commands / and meditate on your statutes. / Remember your word to your servant / since you have given me hope. / *My comfort in my affliction is / that your promise gives me life.* / Though the proud scoff bitterly at me, / I turn not away from your law. / I remember your ordinances of old, O Lord, / and I am comforted. / Indignation seizes me because of the wicked / who forsake your law. / Your statutes are the theme of my song / in the place of my exile. / By night I remember your name, O Lord, / and I will keep your law. / This I have had, / that I have observed your precepts. / I have said, O Lord, that my part / is to keep your words. / *I entreat you with all my heart, / have pity on me according to your promise.* / I considered my ways / and turned my feet to your decrees. / I was prompt and did not hesitate / in keeping your commands. / Though the snares of the wicked are twined about me / your law I have not forgotten. / At midnight I rise to give you thanks / because of your just ordinances. / I am the companion of all who fear you / and keep your precepts. / Of your kindness, O Lord, the earth is full; / teach me your statutes. / You have done good to your servant, / O Lord, according to your word. / Teach me wisdom and knowledge, / for in your commands I trust. / *Before I was afflicted I went astray, / but now I hold to your promise.* / You are good and bountiful; / teach me your statutes. / Though the proud forge lies against me, / with all my heart I will observe your precepts. / Their heart has become gross and fat; / as for me, your law is my delight. / It is good for me that I have been afflicted, / that I may learn your statutes. / The law of your mouth is to me more precious / than thousands of gold and silver pieces. / Your hands have made me and fashioned me; / give me discernment that I may learn your commands. / *Those who fear you shall see me and be glad, / because I hope in your word.* / I know, O Lord, that your ordinances are just, / and in your faithfulness you have afflicted me. / Let your kindness comfort me / according to your promise to your servants. / Let your compassion come to me that I may live, / for your law is my delight. / Let the proud be put to shame for oppressing me unjustly; / I will meditate on your precepts. / Let those turn to me who fear you / and acknowledge your decrees. / Let my heart be perfect in your statutes, / that I be not put to shame. / *My soul pines for your salvation; / I hope in your word.* / My eyes strain after your promise; / when will you comfort me? / Though I am shriveled like a leathern flask in the smoke, / I have not forgotten your statutes. / How many are the days of your servant? / When will you do judgment on my persecutors? / The proud have dug pits for me; / this is against your law. / All your commands are steadfast; / they persecute me wrongfully; help me! / They have all but put an end to me on the earth, / but I have not forsaken your precepts. / In your kindness give me life, / that I may keep the decrees of your mouth. / Your word, O Lord, endures forever; / it is firm as the heavens. / Through all generations your truth endures; / you have established the earth, and it stands firm: / According to your ordinances they still stand firm: / all things serve you. / Had not your law been my delight, / I should have perished in my affliction. / Never will I forget your precepts, / for through them you gave me life. / *I am yours; save me, / for I have sought your precepts.* / Sinners wait to destroy me, / but I pay heed to your decrees. / I see that all fulfillment has its limits; / broad indeed is your command. / How I love your law, O Lord! / It is my meditation all the day. / Your command has made me wiser than my enemies, / for it is ever with me. / I have more understanding than all my teachers / when your decrees are my meditation. / I have more discernment than the elders, / because I observe your precepts. / *From every evil way I withhold my feet, / that I may keep your words.* / From your ordinances I turn not away, / for you have instructed me. / How sweet to my palate are your promises, / sweeter than honey to my mouth! / Through your precepts I gain discernment; / therefore I hate every false way. / *A lamp to my feet is your word, / a light to my path.* / I resolve and swear / to keep your just ordinances. / I am very much afflicted; / O Lord, give me life according to your word. / Accept, O Lord, the free homage of my mouth, / and teach me your decrees. / Though constantly I take my life in my hands, / yet I forget not your law. / The wicked have laid a snare for me, / but from your precepts I have not strayed. / Your decrees are my inheritance forever; / the joy of my heart they are. / I intend in my heart to fulfill your statutes / always, to the letter. / I hate men of divided heart, / but I love your law. / You are my refuge and my shield; / in your word I hope. / Depart from me, you wrongdoers, / and I will observe the commands of my God. / *Sustain me as you have promised, that I may live; / disappoint me not in my hope.* / Help me, that I may be safe / and ever delight in your statutes. / You despise all who stray from your statutes, / for their deceitfulness is in vain. / You account all the wicked of the earth as dross; / therefore I love your decrees. / My flesh shudders with dread of you, / and I fear your ordinances. / I have fulfilled just ordinances; / leave me not to my oppressors. / Be surety for the welfare of your servant; / let not the proud oppress me. / *My eyes strain after your salvation / and your just promise.* / Deal with your servant according to your kindness, / and teach me your statutes. / I am your servant; give me discernment / that I may know your decrees. / It is time for the Lord to act: / they have broken your law. / For I love your command / more than gold, however fine. / For in all your precepts I go forward; / every false way I hate. / Wonderful are your decrees; / therefore I observe them. / The revelation of your words sheds light, / giving understanding to the simple. / I gasp with open mouth / in my yearning for your commands. / Turn to me in pity / as you turn to those who love your name. / Steady my footsteps according to your promise, / and let no iniquity rule over me. / Redeem me from the oppression of men, / that I may keep your precepts. / *Let your countenance shine upon your servant, / and teach me your statutes.* / My eyes shed streams of tears / because your law has not been kept. / You are just, O Lord, / and your ordinance is right. / You have pronounced your decrees in justice / and in perfect faithfulness. / My zeal consumes me, / because my foes forget your words. / *Your promise is very sure, / and your servant loves it.* / I am mean and contemptible, / but your precepts I have not forgotten. / Your justice is everlasting justice, / and your law is permanent. / Though distress and anguish have come upon me, / your commands are my delight. / Your decrees are forever just; / give me discernment that I may live. / I call out with all my heart; answer me, O Lord; / I will observe your statutes. / I call upon you; save me, / and I will keep your decrees. / *Before dawn I come and cry out; / I hope in your words. / My eyes greet the night watches / in meditation on your promise.* / Hear my voice according to your kindness, O Lord; / according to your ordinance give me life. / I am attacked by malicious persecutors / who are far from your law. / You, O Lord, are near, / and all your commands are permanent. / Of old I know from your decrees, / that you have established them forever. / Behold my affliction, and rescue me, / for I have not forgotten your law. / *Plead my cause, and redeem me; / for the sake of your promise give me life.* / Far from sinners is salvation, / because they seek not your statutes. / Your compassion is great, O Lord; / according to your ordinances give me life. / Though my persecutors and my foes are many, / I turn not away from your decrees. / I beheld the apostates with loathing, / because they kept not to your promise. / See how I love your precepts, O Lord; / in your kindness give me life. / Permanence is your word's chief trait; / each of your just ordinances is everlasting. / Princes persecute me without cause / but my heart stands in awe of your word. / I rejoice at your promise, / as one who has found rich spoil. / Falsehood I hate and abhor; / your law I love. / Seven times a day I praise you / for your just ordinances. / *Those who love your law have great peace, / and for them there is no stumbling block.* / I wait for your salvation, O Lord, / and your commands I fulfill. / I keep your decrees / and love them deeply. / I keep your precepts and your decrees, / for all my ways are before you. / Let my cry come before you, O Lord; / in keeping with your word, give me discernment. / Let my supplication reach you; / rescue me according to your promise. / My lips pour forth your praise, / because you teach me your statutes. / May my tongue sing of your promise, / for all your commands are just. / Let your hand be ready to help me, / for I have chosen your precepts. / *I long for your salvation, O Lord, / and your law is my delight.* / Let my soul live to praise you, / and may your ordinances heal me. / I have gone astray [like a lost sheep]; seek your servant, / because your commands I do not forget. (Ps 119)

## 34. To Guide Us to Salvation

God cannot be outdone in generosity. In his creating and caring love, he has literally given us everything. These gifts, great as they are, are only a dim shadow of the greatest gift he has in store for us—our union with him for an eternity of perfect love, peace, and joy. "It is owing to his favor that salvation is yours through faith. This is not your own doing, it is God's gift; neither is it a reward for anything you have accomplished" (Eph 2:8-9a).

**A Caring Shepherd.** "May the Lord, the God of the spirits of all mankind, set over the community a man who shall act as their leader in all things, to guide them in all their actions; that the Lord's community may not be like sheep without a shepherd." (Nm 27:16-17)

**Blessed Wood.** For blest is the wood through which justice comes about. (Wis 14:7)

**We Belong to You.** But you, our God, are good and true, / slow to anger, and governing all with mercy. / For even if we sin we are yours, and know your might; / but we will not sin, knowing that we belong to you. / For to know you well is complete justice, / and to know your might is the root of immortality. (Wis 15:1-3)

**Like Gentle Rain.** Let justice descend, O heavens, like dew from above, / like gentle rain let the skies drop it down. / Let the earth open and salvation bud forth; / let justice also spring up! (Is 45:8)

**Have No Fear.** You heard me call, "Let not your ear / be deaf to my cry for help!" / You came to my aid when I called to you; / you said, "Have no fear!"

You defended me in mortal danger, / you redeemed my life. / You see, O Lord, how I am wronged; / do me justice! / You see all their vindictiveness, / all their plots against me. / You hear their insults, O Lord, / [all their plots against me], / The whispered murmurings of my foes, / against me all the day; / Whether they sit or stand, / see, I am their taunt song. (Lam 3:56-63)

**God's Promise.** *O God, by your name save me, / and by your might defend my cause. / O God, hear my prayer; / hearken to the words of my mouth.* / For haughty men have risen up against me, / and fierce men seek my life; / they set not God before their eyes. / Behold, God is my helper; / the Lord sustains my life. / Turn back the evil upon my foes; / in your faithfulness destroy them. / Freely will I offer you sacrifice: / I will praise your name, O Lord, for its goodness, / Because from all distress you have rescued me, / and my eyes look down upon my enemies. (Ps 54)

**Our Deliverer.** Deign, O God, to rescue me; / O Lord, make haste to help me. / Let them be put to shame and confounded / who seek my life. / Let them be turned back in disgrace / who desire my ruin. / Let them retire in their shame / who say to me, "Aha, aha!" / *But may all who seek you / exult and be glad in you, / And may those who love your salvation / say ever, "God be glorified!"* / But I am afflicted and poor; / O God, hasten to me! / You are my help and my deliverer; / O Lord, hold not back! (Ps 70)

**Divine Aid.** *O God, do not remain unmoved; / be not silent, O God, and be not still!* / For behold, your enemies raise a tumult, / and they who hate you lift up their heads. / Against your people they plot craftily; / they conspire against those whom you protect. / They say, "Come, let us destroy their nation; / let the name of Israel be remembered no more!" / Yes, they consult together with one mind, / and against you they are allied: / The tents of Edom and the Ishmaelites, / Moab and the people of Hagar, / Gebal and Ammon and Amalek, / Philistia with the inhabitants of Tyre; / The Assyrians, too, are leagued with them; / they are the forces of the sons of Lot. / Deal with them as with Midian; / as with Sisera and Jabin at the torrent Kishon, / Who perished at Endor; / they became dung on the ground. / Make their nobles like Oreb and Zeeb; / all their chiefs like Zebah and Zalmunna, / Who said, "Let us take for ourselves / the dwelling place of God." / O my God, make them like leaves in a whirlwind, / like chaff before the wind. / As a fire raging in a forest, / as a flame setting the mountains ablaze, / So pursue them with your tempest / and rout them with your storm. / Darken their faces with disgrace, / that men may seek your name, O Lord. / *Let them be shamed and put to rout forever; / let them be confounded and perish, / Knowing that you alone are the Lord, / the Most High over all the earth.* (Ps 83)

## 35. To Strengthen Our Commitment

We are told that love can do the hard things immediately, but it takes just a little longer to do the impossible. There is much truth in that adage. We cannot make a firm commitment to the Lord unless we love him. Mary was "madly" in love with God, hence she could make her total commitment without hesitation. Her example is motivating: "I am the servant of the Lord. Let it be done to me as you say" (Lk 1:38).

**I Do Believe.** "Yes, Lord, I have come to believe that you are the Messiah, the Son of God: he who is to come into the world." (Jn 11:27)

**His Call.** We pray for you always that our God may make you worthy of his call, and fulfill by his power every honest intention and work of faith. (2 Thes 1:11)

**Yes, Lord.** "I have come to do your will, O God." (Heb 10:7b)

**In His Service.** To him who loves us and freed us from our sins by his own blood, who has made us a royal nation of priests in the service of his God and Father—to him be glory and power forever and ever! Amen. (Rv 1:5b-6)

**Happy the Man.** *Happy the man who follows not / the counsel of the wicked / Nor walks in the way of sinners, / nor sits in the company of the insolent, / But delights in the law of the Lord / and meditates on his law day and night. /* He is like a tree / planted near running water, / That yields its fruit in due season, / and whose leaves never fade. / [Whatever he does, prospers.] / Not so the wicked, not so; / they are like chaff which the wind drives away. / Therefore in judgment the wicked shall not stand, / nor shall sinners, in the assembly of the just. / For the Lord watches over the way of the just, / but the way of the wicked vanishes. (Ps 1)

**False Happiness.** How good God is to the upright; / the Lord, to those who are clean of heart! / But, as for me, I almost lost my balance; / my feet all but slipped, / Because I was envious of the arrogant / when I saw them prosper though they were wicked. / For they are in no pain; / their bodies are sound and sleek; / They are free from the burdens of mortals, / and are not afflicted like the rest of men. / So pride adorns them as a necklace; / as a robe violence enwraps them. / Out of their crassness comes iniquity; / their fancies overflow their hearts. / They scoff and speak evil; / outrage from on high they threaten. / They set their mouthings in place of heaven, / and their pronouncements roam the earth: / "So he brings his people to such a pass / that they have not even water!" / And they say, "How does God know?" / And, "Is there any knowledge in the Most High?" / Such, then, are the wicked; / always carefree, while they increase in wealth. / Is it but in vain I have kept my heart clean / and washed my hands as an innocent man? / For I suffer affliction day after day / and chastisement with each new dawn. / Had I thought, "I will speak as they do," / I had been false to the fellowship of your children. / Though I tried to understand this / it seemed to me too difficult, / Till I entered the sanctuary of God / and considered their final destiny. / You set them, indeed, on a slippery road; / you hurl them down to ruin. / How suddenly they are made desolate! / They are completely wasted away amid horrors. / As though they were the dream of one who had awakened, O Lord, / so will you, when you arise, set at nought these phantoms. / Because my heart was embittered / and my soul was pierced, / I was stupid and understood not; / I was like a brute beast in your presence. / *Yet with you I shall always be: / you have hold of my right hand; / With your counsel you guide me, / and in the end you will receive me in glory. / Whom else have I in heaven? / And when I am with you, the earth delights me not.* / Though my flesh and my heart waste away, / God is the rock of my heart and my portion forever. / For indeed, they who withdraw from you perish; / you destroy everyone who is unfaithful to you. / But for me, to be near God is my good; / to make the Lord God my refuge. / I shall declare all your works / in the gates of the daughter of Zion. (Ps 73)

**Walk in Integrity.** Of kindness and judgment I will sing; / to you, O Lord, I will sing praise. / *I will persevere in the way of integrity; / when will you come to me? / I will walk in the integrity of my heart, / within my house; / I will not set before my eyes / any base thing. / I hate him who does perversely; / he shall not remain with me.* / A crooked heart shall be far from me; / evil I will not know. / Whoever slanders his neighbor in secret, / him will I destroy. / The man of haughty eyes and puffed-up heart / I will not endure. / My eyes are upon the faithful of the land, / that they may dwell with me. / He who walks in the way of integrity / shall be in my service. / He shall not dwell within my house / who practices deceit. / He who speaks falsehood shall not stand / before my eyes. / Each morning I will destroy / all the wicked of the land, / And uproot from the city of the Lord / all evildoers. (Ps 101)

**Genuine Happiness.** *Happy the man who fears the Lord, / who greatly delights in his commands.* / His posterity shall be mighty upon the earth; / the upright generation shall be blessed. / Wealth and riches shall be in his house; / his generosity shall endure forever. / *He dawns through the darkness, a light for the upright; / he is gracious and merciful and just.* / Well for the man who is gracious and lends, / who conducts his affairs with justice; / He shall never be moved; / the just man shall be in everlasting remembrance. / An evil report he shall not fear; / his heart is firm, trusting in the Lord. / His heart is steadfast; he shall not fear / till he looks down upon his foes. / Lavishly he gives to the poor; / his generosity shall endure forever, / his horn shall be exalted in glory. / The wicked man shall see it and be vexed; / he shall gnash his teeth and pine away; / the desire of the wicked shall perish. (Ps 112)

## 36. *To Say Thank You*

In his public ministry Jesus paused many times to say thank you to his Father. He likewise manifested his disappointment at the lack of gratitude of the nine lepers. A prayerful person will be a grateful person. We need to ask ourselves what have we that has not been given to us; then we will be grateful. St. Paul advises, "Whatever you do, whether in speech or in action, do it in the name of the Lord Jesus. Give thanks to God the Father through him" (Col 3:17).

**Grateful Heart.** I give you thanks, O God of my father; / I praise you, O God my savior! / I will make known your name, refuge of my life. (Sir 51:1)

**I Give Thanks.** I give you thanks, O Lord; / though you have been angry with me, / your anger has abated, and you have consoled me. / God indeed is my savior; / I am confident and unafraid. / My strength and my courage is the Lord, / and he has been my savior.

With joy you will draw water / at the fountain of salvation, and say on that day: / Give thanks to the Lord, acclaim his name; / among the nations make known his deeds, / proclaim how exalted is his name. / Sing praise to the Lord for his glorious achievement; / let this be known throughout all the earth. (Is 12:1b-5)

**Glorious Deeds.** The favors of the Lord I will recall, / the glorious deeds of the Lord, / Because of all he has done for us; / for he is good to the house of Israel, / He has favored us according to his mercy / and his great kindness. (Is 63:7)

**Look Redeemed.** [Give] thanks to the Father for having made you worthy to share the lot of the saints in light. He rescued us from the power of darkness and brought us into the kingdom of his beloved Son. Through him we have redemption, the forgiveness of our sins. (Col 1:12-14)

**Grateful for Victory.** *I will give thanks to you, O Lord, with all my heart; / I will declare all your wondrous deeds. / I will be glad and exult in you; / I will sing praise to your name, Most High,* / Because my enemies are turned back, / overthrown and destroyed before you. / For you upheld my right and my cause / seated on your throne, judging justly. / You rebuked the nations and destroyed the wicked; / their name you blotted out forever and ever. / The enemies are ruined completely forever; / the remembrance of the cities you uprooted has perished. / But the Lord sits enthroned forever; / he has set up his throne for judgment. / He judges the world with justice; / he governs the peoples with equity. / The Lord is a stronghold for the oppressed, / a stronghold in times of distress. / They trust in you who cherish your name, / for you forsake not those who seek you, O Lord. / Sing praise to the Lord enthroned in Zion; / proclaim among the nations his deeds; / For the avenger of blood has remembered; / he has not forgotten the cry of the afflicted. / Have pity on me, O Lord; see how I am afflicted by my foes, / you who have raised me up from the gates of death, / That I may declare all your praises / and, in the gates of the daughter of Zion, / rejoice in your salvation. / The nations are sunk in the pit they have made; / in the snare they set, their foot is caught; / In passing sentence, the Lord is manifest; / the wicked are trapped by the work of their own hands. / To the nether world the wicked shall turn back, / all the nations that forget God. / For the needy shall not always be forgotten, / nor shall the hope of the afflicted forever perish. / Rise, O Lord, let no man prevail; / let the nations be judged in your presence. / Strike them with terror, O Lord; / let the nations know that they are but men. (Ps 9)

**We Thank You.** O Lord, in your strength the king is glad; / in your victory how greatly he rejoices! / You have granted him his heart's desire; / you refused not the wish of his lips. / For you welcomed him with goodly blessings, / you placed on his head a crown of pure gold. / He asked life of you: you gave him / length of days forever and ever. / Great is his glory in your victory; / majesty and splendor you conferred upon him. / For you made him a blessing forever; / you gladdened him with the joy of your presence. / For the king trusts in the Lord, / and through the kindness of the Most High he stands unshaken. / May your hand reach all your enemies, / may your right hand reach your foes! / Make them burn as though in a fiery furnace, / when you appear. / May the Lord consume them in his anger; / let fire devour them. / Destroy their fruit from the earth / and their posterity from among men. / Though they intend evil against you, / devising plots, they cannot succeed, / For you shall put them to flight; / you shall aim your shafts against them. / *Be extolled, O Lord, in your strength! / We will sing, chant the praise of your might.* (Ps 21)

**Appreciating Good Health.** I will extol you, O Lord, for you drew me clear / and did not let my enemies rejoice over me. / O Lord, my God, / I cried out to you and you healed me. / O Lord, you brought me up from the nether world; / you preserved me from among those going down into the pit. / *Sing praise to the Lord, you his faithful ones, / and give thanks to his holy name. / For his anger lasts but a moment; / a lifetime, his good will. / At nightfall, weeping enters in, / but with the dawn, rejoicing.* / Once, in my security, I said, / "I shall never be disturbed." / O Lord, in your good will you had endowed me with majesty and strength: / but when you hid your face I was terrified. / To you, O Lord, I cried out; / with the Lord I pleaded: / "What gain would there be from my life-blood, / from my going down into the grave? / Would dust give you thanks / or proclaim your faithfulness? / Hear, O Lord, and have pity on me; / O Lord, be my helper." / You changed my mourning into dancing; / you took off my sackcloth and clothed me with gladness, / That my soul might sing praise to you without ceasing; / O Lord, my God, forever will I give you thanks. (Ps 30)

**Gratitude for Success.** Great is the Lord and wholly to be praised / in the city of our God. / His holy mountain, fairest of heights, / is the joy of all the earth; / Mount Zion, "the recesses of the North," / is the city of the great King. / God is with her castles; / renowned is he as a stronghold. / For lo! the kings assemble, / they come on together; / They also see, and at once are stunned, / terrified, routed; / Quaking seizes them there; / anguish, like a woman's in labor, / As though a wind from the east / were shattering ships of Tarshish. / As we ad heard, so have we seen / in the city of the Lord of hosts, / In the city of our God; / God makes it firm forever. / O God, we ponder your kindness / within your temple. / *As your name, O God, so also your praise / reaches to the ends of the earth. / Of justice your right hand is full;* / let Mount Zion be glad, / Let the cities of Judah rejoice, / because of your judgments. / Go about Zion, make the round; / count her towers. / Consider her ramparts, / examine her castles, / That you may tell a future generation / that such is God, / Our God forever and ever; / he will guide us. (Ps 48)

**Grateful Hearts.** *I will give thanks to you, O Lord, with all my heart, / [for you have heard the words of my mouth;] / in the presence of the angels I will sing your praise; / I will worship at your holy temple / and give thanks to your name, / Because of your kindness and your truth; / for you have made great above all things / your name and your promise.* / When I called, you answered me; / you built up strength within me. / All the kings of the earth shall give thanks to you, O Lord, / when they hear the words of your mouth; / And they shall sing of the ways of the Lord: / "Great is the glory of the Lord." / The Lord is exalted, yet the lowly he sees, / and the proud he knows from afar. / Though I walk amid distress, you preserve me; / against the anger of my enemies you raise your hand; / your right hand saves me. / The Lord will complete what he has done for me; / your kindness, O Lord, endures forever; / forsake not the work of your hands. (Ps 138)

## 37. To Sing His Praises

Praise is a high form of prayer, since it focuses on God himself rather than on his gifts. Praising God gives us a joy and exuberance that naturally breaks into song. In praising God we often multiply words in an attempt to describe him and all his grandeur and greatness. "Sing to the Lord a new song, / his praise from the end of the earth: / Let the sea and what fills it resound, / the coastlands, and those who dwell in them" (Is 42:10).

**Blessed Be God.** Blessed be God who lives forever, / because his kingdom lasts for all ages. / For he scourges and then has mercy; / he casts down to the depths of the nether world, / and he brings up from the great abyss. / No one can escape his hand. . . .

Exalt him before every living being, / because he is the Lord our God, / our Father and God forever. . . .

When you turn back to him with all your heart, / to do what is right before him, / Then he will turn back to you, / and no longer hide his face from you.

So now consider what he has done for you, / and praise him with full voice. / Bless the Lord of righteousness, / and exalt the King of the ages. / In the land of my exile I praise him, / and show his power and majesty to a sinful nation. . . .

"As for me, I exalt my God, / and my spirit rejoices in the King of heaven. / Let all men speak of his majesty, / and sing his praises in Jerusalem." (Tb 13:1-2, 4, 6-8)

**Bless God.** And now, bless the God of all, / who has done wondrous things on earth; / Who fosters men's growth from their mother's womb, / and fashions them according to his will! / May he grant you joy of heart / and may peace abide among you. (Sir 50:22-23)

**Faithful and True.** O Lord, you are my God, / I will extol you and praise your name; / For you have fulfilled your wonderful plans of old, / faithful and true. (Is 25:1)

**Hosanna.** "Hosanna to the Son of David! / Blessed is he who comes in the name of the Lord! / Hosanna in the highest!" (Mt 21:9b)

**King of Ages.** To the King of ages, the immortal, the invisible, the only God, be honor and glory forever and ever! Amen. (1 Tm 1:17)

**All Glory.** *The heavens declare the glory of God, / and the firmament proclaims his handiwork.* / Day pours out the word to day, / and night to night imparts knowledge; / Not a word nor a discourse / whose voice is not heard; / Through all the earth their voice resounds, / and to the ends of the world, their message. / He has pitched a tent there for the sun, / which comes forth like the groom from his bridal chamber / and, like a giant, joyfully runs its course. / At one end of the heavens it comes forth, / and its course is to their other end; / nothing escapes its heat. / The law of the Lord is perfect, / refreshing the soul; / The decree of the Lord is trustworthy, / giving wisdom to the simple. / The precepts of the Lord are right, / rejoicing the heart; / The command of the Lord is clear, / enlightening the eye; / The fear of the Lord is pure, / enduring forever; / The ordinances of the Lord are true, / all of them just; / They are more precious than gold, / than a heap of purest gold; / Sweeter also than syrup / or honey from the comb. / Though your servant is careful of them, / very diligent in keeping them, / Yet who can detect failings? / Cleanse me from my unknown faults! / From wanton sin especially, restrain your servant; / let it not rule over me. / Then shall I be blameless and innocent / of serious sin. / *Let the words of my mouth and the thought of my heart / find favor before you, / O Lord, my rock and my redeemer.* (Ps 19)

**God's Majesty.** *Give to the Lord, you sons of God, / give to the Lord glory and praise, / Give to the Lord the glory due his name,* / adore the Lord in holy attire. /The voice of the Lord is over the waters, / the God of glory thunders, / the Lord, over vast waters. / The voice of the Lord is mighty; / the voice of the Lord is majestic. / The voice of the Lord breaks the cedars, / the Lord breaks the cedars of Lebanon. / He makes Lebanon leap like a calf / and Sirion like a young bull. / The voice of the Lord strikes fiery flames; / the voice of the Lord shakes the desert, / the Lord shakes the wilderness of Kadesh. / The voice of the Lord twists the oaks and strips the forests, / and in his temple all say, "Glory!" / The Lord is enthroned above the flood; / the Lord is enthroned as king forever. / May the Lord give strength to his people; / may the Lord bless his people with peace! (Ps 29)

**Sacrifice of Praise.** God the Lord has spoken and summoned the earth, / from the rising of the sun to its setting. / From Zion, perfect in beauty, / God shines forth. / May our God come and not be deaf to us! / Before him is a devouring fire; / round him is a raging storm. / He summons the heavens from above, / and the earth, to the trial of his people: / "Gather my faithful ones before me, / those who have made a covenant with me by sacrifice." / And the heavens proclaim his justice;

/ for God himself is the judge. / "Hear, my people, and I will speak; / Israel, I will testify against you; / God, your God, am I. / Not for your sacrifices do I rebuke you, / for your holocausts are before me always. / I take from your house no bullock, / no goats out of your fold. / For mine are all the animals of the forests, / beasts by the thousand on my mountains. / I know all the birds of the air, / and whatever stirs in the plains, belongs to me. / If I were hungry, I should not tell you, / for mine are the world and its fullness. / Do I eat the flesh of strong bulls, / or is the blood of goats my drink? / Offer to God praise as your sacrifice / and fulfill your vows to the Most High; / Then call upon me in time of distress; / I will rescue you, and you shall glorify me." / But to the wicked man God says: / "Why do you recite my statutes, / and profess my covenant with your mouth, / Though you hate discipline / and cast my words behind you? / When you see a thief, you keep pace with him, / and with adulterers you throw in your lot. / To your mouth you give free rein for evil, / you harness your tongue to deceit. / You sit speaking against your brother; / against your mother's son you spread rumors. / When you do these things, shall I be deaf to it? / Or do you think that I am like yourself? / I will correct you by drawing them up before your eyes. / Consider this, you who forget God, / lest I rend you and there be no one to rescue you. / *He that offers praise as a sacrifice glorifies me; / and to him that goes the right way I will show the salvation of God.*" (Ps 50)

**Magnificent Lord.** God arises; his enemies are scattered, / and those who hate him flee before him. / As smoke is driven away, so are they driven; / as wax melts before the fire, / so the wicked perish before God. / But the just rejoice and exult before God; / they are glad and rejoice. / *Sing to God, chant praise to his name, / extol him who rides upon the clouds, / Whose name is the Lord; / exult before him.* / The father of orphans and the defender of widows / is God in his holy dwelling. / God gives a home to the forsaken; / he leads forth prisoners to prosperity; / only rebels remain in the parched land. / O God, when you went forth at the head of your people, / when you marched through the wilderness, / The earth quaked; it rained from heaven at the presence of God, / at the presence of God, the God of Israel, the One of Sinai. / A bountiful rain you showered down, O God, / upon your inheritance; / you restored the land when it languished; / Your flock settled in it; / in your goodness, O God, you provided it for the needy. / The Lord gives the word; / women bear the glad tidings, a vast army: / "Kings and their hosts are fleeing, fleeing, / and the household shall divide the spoils. / Though you rested among the sheepfolds, / the wings of the dove shone with silver, / and her pinions with a golden hue. / While the Almighty dispersed the kings there, / snow fell on Zalmon." / High the mountains of Bashan; / rugged the mountains of Bashan. / Why look you jealously, you rugged mountains, / at the mountain God has chosen for his throne, / where the Lord himself will dwell forever? / The chariots of God are myriad, thousands on thousands; / the Lord advances from Sinai to the sanctuary. / You have ascended on high, taken captives, / received men as gifts— / even rebels; the Lord God enters his dwelling. / Blessed day by day be the Lord, / who bears our burdens; God, who is our salvation. / God is a saving God for us; / the Lord, my Lord, controls the passageways of death. / Surely God crushes the heads of his enemies, / the hairy

crowns of those who stalk about in their guilt. / The
Lord said: "I will fetch them back from Bashan; / I will
fetch them back from the depths of the sea, / So that you
will bathe your feet in blood; / the tongues of your dogs
will have their share of your enemies." / They view your
progress, O God, / the progress of my God, my King,
into the sanctuary; / The singers lead, the minstrels
follow, / in their midst the maidens play on timbrels. / In
your choirs bless God; / bless the Lord, you of Israel's
wellspring! / There is Benjamin, the youngest, leading
them; / the princes of Judah in a body, / the princes of
Zebulun, the princes of Naphtali. / Show forth, O God,
your power, / the power, O God, with which you took
our part; / For your temple in Jerusalem / let the kings
bring you gifts. / Rebuke the wild beast of the reeds; /
the herd of strong bulls and the bullocks, the nations. /
Let them prostrate themselves with bars of silver; /
scatter the peoples who delight in war. / Let nobles come
from Egypt; / let Ethiopia extend its hands to God. / *You
kingdoms of the earth, sing to God, / chant praise to the Lord* /
who rides on the heights of the ancient heavens. /
Behold, his voice resounds, the voice of power: /
"Confess the power of God!" / Over Israel is his majesty;
/ his power is in the skies. / Awesome in his sanctuary is
God, the God of Israel; / he gives power and strength to
his people. / Blessed be God! (Ps 68)

**All Stops Open.** Praise the Lord in his sanctuary, / praise
him in the firmament of his strength. / *Praise him for his
mighty deeds, / praise him for his sovereign majesty.* / Praise
him with the blast of the trumpet, / praise him with lyre
and harp, / Praise him with timbrel and dance, / praise
him with strings and pipe. / Praise him with sounding

cymbals, / praise him with clanging cymbals. / *Let everything that has breath / praise the Lord! Alleluia.* (Ps 150)

## 38. To Give Glory to God

We praise God for himself, but we give him glory for his lofty deeds and his manifestations throughout the ages. The greatest of his manifestations was the Incarnation of his own divine Son as savior and redeemer. How appropriate the angels' song: "Glory to God in high heaven" (Lk 2:14). Jesus, in turn, manifested the glory of the Father. United with Jesus, we too can give God the glory. "For from him and through him and for him all things are. To him be glory forever" (Rom 11:36).

**Lord of Hosts.** "Holy, holy, holy is the Lord of hosts!" . . . "All the earth is filled with his glory!" (Is 6:3)

**In High Heaven.** "Glory to God in high heaven, / peace on earth to those on whom his favor rests." (Lk 2:14)

**Unto Endless Ages.** Now to him who is able to strengthen you in the gospel which I proclaim when I preach Jesus Christ, the gospel which reveals the mystery hidden for many ages but now manifested through the writings of the prophets, and, at the command of the eternal God, made known to all the Gentiles that they may believe and obey—to him, the God who alone is wise, may glory be given through Jesus Christ unto endless ages. Amen. (Rom 16:25-27)

**Holy, Holy, Holy.** "Holy, holy, holy, is the Lord God Almighty, / He who was, and who is, and who is to come!" (Rv 4:8)

**The Glories of God.** Exult, you just, in the Lord; / praise from the upright is fitting. / Give thanks to the Lord on the harp; / with the ten-stringed lyre chant his praises. / Sing to him a new song; / pluck the strings skillfully, with shouts of gladness. / For upright is the word of the Lord, / and all his works are trustworthy. / He loves justice and right; / of the kindness of the Lord the earth is full. / By the word of the Lord the heavens were made; / by the breath of his mouth all their host. / He gathers the waters of the sea as in a flask; / in cellars he confines the deep. / Let all the earth fear the Lord; / let all who dwell in the world revere him. / For he spoke, and it was made; / he commanded, and it stood forth. / The Lord brings to nought the plans of nations; / he foils the designs of peoples. / But the plan of the Lord stands forever; / the design of his heart, through all generations. / Happy the nation whose God is the Lord, / the people he has chosen for his own inheritance. / From heaven the Lord looks down; / he sees all mankind. / From his fixed throne he beholds / all who dwell on the earth, / He who fashioned the heart of each, / he who knows all their works. / A king is not saved by a mighty army, / nor is a warrior delivered by great strength. / Useless is the horse for safety; / great though its strength, it cannot provide escape. / But see, the eyes of the Lord are upon those who fear him, / upon those who hope for his kindness, / To deliver them from death / and preserve them in spite of famine. / *Our soul waits for* *the Lord, / who is our help and our shield, / For in him our hearts rejoice; / in his holy name we trust.* / May your kindness, O Lord, be upon us / who have put our hope in you. (Ps 33)

**His Kindness Endures.** *Sing joyfully to the Lord, all you lands; / serve the Lord with gladness; / come before him with joyful song.* / Know that the Lord is God; / he made us, his we are; / his people, the flock he tends. / Enter his gates with thanksgiving, / his courts with praise; / Give thanks to him; bless his name, for he is good: / the Lord, whose kindness endures forever, / and his faithfulness to all generations. (Ps 100)

**His Mercy Lasts.** *Alleluia. Give thanks to the Lord, for he is good, / for his mercy endures forever;* / Give thanks to the God of gods, / for his mercy endures forever; / Give thanks to the Lord of lords, / for his mercy endures forever; / Who alone does great wonders, / for his mercy endures forever; / Who made the heavens in wisdom, / for his mercy endures forever; / Who spread out the earth upon the waters, / for his mercy endures forever; / Who made the great lights, / for his mercy endures forever; / The sun to rule over the day, / for his mercy endures forever; / The moon and the stars to rule over the night, / for his mercy endures forever; / Who smote the Egyptians in their first-born, / for his mercy endures forever; / And brought out Israel from their midst, / for his mercy endures forever; / With a mighty hand and an outstretched arm, / for his mercy endures forever; / Who split the Red Sea in twain, / for his mercy endures forever; / And led Israel through its midst, / for his mercy endures forever; / But swept Pharaoh and his army into the Red Sea, / for his mercy endures forever; / Who led his people through the wilderness, / for his mercy endures forever; / Who smote great kings, / for his mercy endures forever; / And slew powerful kings, / for his mercy endures forever; / Sihon, king of the Amorites, / for his mercy endures forever; /And Og, king of Bashan, / for his mercy endures forever; / And made their land a heritage, / for his mercy endures forever; / The heritage of Israel his servant, / for his mercy endures forever; / Who remembered us in our abjection, / for his mercy endures forever; / And freed us from our foes, / for his mercy endures forever; / Who gives food to all flesh, / for his mercy endures forever; / *Give thanks to the God of heaven, / for his mercy endures forever.* (Ps 136)

**Loving Providence.** *I will extol you, O my God and King, / and I will bless your name forever and ever. / Every day will I bless you, / and I will praise your name forever and ever. /* Great is the Lord and highly to be praised; / his greatness is unsearchable. / Generation after generation praises your works / and proclaims your might. / They speak of the splendor of your glorious majesty / and tell of your wondrous works. / They discourse of the power of your terrible deeds / and declare your greatness. / They publish the fame of your abundant goodness / and joyfully sing of your justice. / The Lord is gracious and merciful, / slow to anger and of great kindness. / The Lord is good to all / and compassionate toward all his works. / *Let all your works give you thanks, O Lord, / and let your faithful ones bless you. / Let them discourse of the glory of your kingdom / and speak of your might,* / Making known to men your might / and the glorious splendor of your kingdom. / Your kingdom is a kingdom for all ages, /

and your dominion endures through all generations. /
The Lord is faithful in all his words / and holy in all his
works. / The Lord lifts up all who are falling / and raises
up all who are bowed down. / The eyes of all look
hopefully to you, / and you give them their food in due
season; / You open your hand / and satisfy the desire of
every living thing. / The Lord is just in all his ways / and
holy in all his works. / The Lord is near to all who call
upon him, / to all who call upon him in truth. / He
fulfills the desire of those who fear him, / he hears their
cry and saves them. / The Lord keeps all who love him, /
but all the wicked he will destroy. / May my mouth speak
the praise of the Lord, / and may all flesh bless his holy
name forever and ever. (Ps 145)

**Exult in Glory.** *Sing to the Lord a new song / of praise in the
assembly of the faithful.* / Let Israel be glad in their maker,
/ let the children of Zion rejoice in their king. / Let them
praise his name in the festive dance, / let them sing praise
to him with timbrel and harp. / For the Lord loves his
people, / and he adorns the lowly with victory. / *Let the
faithful exult in glory; / let them sing for joy upon their
couches; / let the high praises of God be in their throats. / And
let two-edged swords be in their hands:* / to execute
vengeance on the nations, / punishments on the peoples;
/ To bind their kings with chains, / their nobles with
fetters of iron; / To execute on them the written
sentence. / This is the glory of all his faithful. Alleluia.
(Ps 149)

# The Magnificat

Mary invites us to praise God daily with her:

"My being proclaims the greatness of the Lord, / my spirit finds joy in God my savior, / For he has looked upon his servant in her lowliness; / all ages to come shall call me blessed. / God who is mighty has done great things for me, / holy is his name; / His mercy is from age to age / on those who fear him.

"He has shown might with his arm; / he has confused the proud in their inmost thoughts. / He has deposed the mighty from their thrones / and raised the lowly to high places. / The hungry he has given every good thing, / while the rich he has sent empty away. / He has upheld Israel his servant, / ever mindful of his mercy; / Even as he promised our fathers, / promised Abraham and his descendants forever." (Lk 1:46-55)

# Index

## NEW TESTAMENT
Includes references from Chapter 1 and Chapter 3